"Judy Slater has produced a brilliant, creative, thoughtful, and extren
to self-love and self-fulfillment. This is a foundational tool invaluable
committed to their personal growth."

Interfaith Cou... ...g Center, San Anselmo

"Self-Wonderful is magical in its potential to change people's lives. In my work as an Intuitive Healer, the lack of self-love is often the primary issue that leads to chronic illness. I can recommend this resource to my clients to help them reach their health goals."

Connie Prodromou, L.AC., MIM®

"What I love about Judy's remarkable book is the belief that self-love is the path to a fulfilling life. What's great are the tangible things to do to experience this self-love...and who does not want that!"

Dr. Rick Tamlyn, MCC, CPCC, Hay House author of "Play Your Bigger Game

"I love it when I see a good card deck."

Nick Kellet, Founder Deckibles.com

"What Judy has developed and put together with her book is beyond impressive and useful. Judy invites her readers to access, explore, and reflect on their "self-wonderfulness" from many viewpoints with warmth, heart, wisdom, and playfulness. I think this book is accessible to everyone and I would not hesitate to recommend this book to any mental health or life coach professional, as well."

Paul Puccinelli, LMFT, MA

"As a physician for 25 years, I've observed that for many of my patients who come to me exhausted and fatigued, they haven't developed the energetic channels to receive. There is a tendency to give and give and give till depletion arrives at the front door and one is forced to slow down from a health crisis. I often tell my patients, 'One of the biggest mistakes you can make is to continue to give and not receive as you regain your energy.' I've often wanted a simple manual one could turn to in order to learn the principles of self-love, especially if there is not the time available for a silent retreat, spa vacation, or hours of weekly therapy. Judy has created a lovely manual and card deck that help guide a person into practices of self-love. Her book "The Simply Self-Wonderful Inner Workout Book" teaches you the art of receiving in a concise, thorough, yet playful way. This is pivotal for someone who wants to live a long healthy and fulfilling life.

Dr. Jacqueline Susanna Chan, DO, MIM®

"*The Simply Self-Wonderful Inner Workout Book* and card deck by Judy Slater is an incredibly vast collection of affirmations, exercises, and messages that one can use to remind themselves that they are a special gift to the world. I love the way Judy presents it as a way to reaffirm who you are and what your purpose in this life is because of your uniqueness. Judy gives many resources for those who wish to delve deeper into the topic. Self-Wonderful is magical in its potential to change people's lives. In my work as an Intuitive Healer, the lack of self-love is often the primary issue that leads to chronic illness so here is a resource that I can recommend to my clients that can help them reach their health goals."

Connie Prodromou, L.Ac., MIM®

"Fantastic- creative, unique, and powerful!"

Sydney Wiecking CPCC, MCC Personal, Executive and Leadership Coach

"Thought-provoking and motivating! Judy's deck and workbook provide so many opportunities to reflect upon, grow from and learn…especially when you have teenagers. Our relationship with ourselves and others is key and Judy's personal touch in helping you to find your way is invaluable."

Diane Gasson, Mom of Two Teen Girls

The Simply Self-Wonderful Inner Workout Book

Celebrating the Gifts of Being Uniquely You

by Judy E. Slater

Published by
Hybrid Global Publishing
333 E 14th Street
#3C
New York, NY 10003

Manufactured in the United States of America, or in the United Kingdom when distributed elsewhere.

Slater, Judy E.
The Simply Self-Wonderful Inner Workout Book
ISBN: 978-1-961757-01-1
eBook: 978-1-961757-02-8
Card Deck: 978-1-961757-03-5
Book & Card Deck Bundle: 978-1-961757-04-2
LCCN: 2023913617

Cover design by: Anne Dunnett
Copyediting by: Wendie Pecharsky
Interior design by: Suba Murugan
Illustrator: Tanya Back
Author photo by: Danny Dek

www.simplyselfwonderful.com

To YOU, readers, who are Simply Self-Wonderful
And to Charles – Because You Loved Me

Table of Contents

Self-Wonderfuls

Self - Acceptance
Self - Actualization
Self - Appreciation
Self - Assurance
Self - Aware
Self - Care
Self - Celebration
Self - Compassion
Self - Confidence
Self - Conscious
Self - Determination
Self - Discipline
Self - Discovery
Self - Efficacy
Self - Empowerment
Self - Esteem
Self - Expression
Self - Fulfillment
Self - Image
Self - Love
Self - Portrait
Self - Possessed
Self - Preservation
Self - Reflection
Self - Regard
Self - Reliance
Self - Respect
Self - Starter
Self - Trust
Self - Understanding
Self - Worth
Selfless

Self-Woundings

Self - Absorption
Self - Abuse
Self - Centered
Self - Condemnation
Self - Criticism
Self - Deception
Self - Defeat
Self - Denial
Self - Deprecation
Self - Destruction
Self - Doubt
Self - Effacing
Self - Flattery
Self - Gratification
Self - Harm
Self - Humiliation
Self - Imposed
Self - Indulgence
Self - Inflicted
Self - Involved
Self - Judgment
Self - Licensing
Self - Loathing
Self - Pity
Self - Pride
Self - Punishment
Self - Righteous
Self - Sabotage
Self - Sufficiency
Self - Torment
Selfish

Acknowledgements

Coming as an intuitive hit from the interconnected benevolent universe, calling and saying, 'I want this in the world', The Simply Self-Wonderful Card Deck and Inner Workout Book includes everyone and everything that came before, thus making it difficult to tease out particulars to name. And yet, there were bright, supportive stars shining every step of the way. It is to you I offer appreciation, gratitude, and thankfulness.

Amy Leavenworth, you offered 'self-wonderfuls' in our healing sessions and sparked a concept and name for the book as card deck and well as deep healing; Marcy Nelson-Garrison your absolutely essential Card Deck Master Class was creatively right-brained and logistically left-brained, and you supported me every step of the way; the Friday morning card deck completion Zoom group Kay Adams, Meredith Brown, Fiona MacEachern and Lorie, your commitment to finishing made it happen; and Tanya Back, you created the whimsical mandalas that brought this dream to life.

Rick Tamlyn, your personal passion and honesty about what it takes to write a book was spot on; the Produce U 2022-2023 fellow book writers Lori Draude, Mike Edwards, Candace Goodwin, Ken Jenkins, Sarah Kenny, Manoj Ramanan V, Alison Scott, and Lynn Young, were big shoes to fill and you showed it was possible; and behind the scenes Chuck Lioi, you held it all together with ease.

Natalie and David Moon-Wainwright, your early support got it started; Dan Christian, your weekly encouraging comments eased my self-doubt; Paul Slaikeu, your exuberant support without hesitation touched my heart; the ICC Tuesday group, your love and 'yes' is heartfelt, Marti Rule, your connections to people and places when I was stuck kept moving me forward; Cheryl Lyon, your humorous spiritual guidance and uplifting spirit kept it possible; Carol Calvert, you see and speak the 'yes' of the Divine creative process; Carol Hovis, your loving, listening, connecting patterns, people, and personalities when triggered emotionally kept me sane; Kathy Runyeon, you offer loving support at any time; Trisha Garrett, your Cuckoo love and affirmation said 'of course'; and Celeste, my neighbor, your 'of course you are a writer, it will happen, you've got higher connections', became my mantra when doubtful.

Beth Law, you were there from the beginning with calm positivity and affirmation; Laura Wilson, you were the editor in the energy space, Jacqueline Chan, Connie Prodromou, TA's, faculty, students at the Academy of Intuition Medicine® and Founder Francesca McCartney, your energy emanates from the book's pages.

The team at Hybrid Global; Karen Strauss, your vision and experience offered a new way to publish a book, Claudia Volkman, you took my words and made them better, Karina Cooke, you dealt with details, logistics, and numbers, Anne Dunnett, you designed the bright and visibly appealing book cover and formatted the variety of content to make each stand out in its own right; Mike Williams and Skylar Destifino at Shuffled Ink, you made sure that everything was as perfect as it could be; Laurie O-Hara, you crunched the numbers and offered business guidance and wisdom when there was major uncertainty near the end; Brian Kraker, you easily create and update my websites; Jennifer Lee, your connections with Nicole Piar's course on Crowdfunding Essentials were invaluable.

And finally, my clients, your commitment to growth and transformation inspires me; and my weekly writing recipients, you let me speak my voice in too many words and still stay subscribed, reading, and wanting more. You are all Simply Self-Wonderful!

Welcome!

It's not strange or impossible to love yourself with all your heart. It's absolutely essential! What matters is that you make it a priority.

The longest relationship you will have in your life is the one with yourself! And at this point in your life, you know and experience what your relationship is like! And I imagine, since you are reading this introduction, you have a deep yearning for something better. You want to feel Simply Self-Wonderful, perhaps not all the time but at least most of the time, and to know ways to get back to being Simply Self-Wonderful so you can live the life you want and create for yourself.

Self-love isn't always easy. There's no self-love destination. It's an ongoing journey you take with yourself. And self-love doesn't demand perfection either. Just trying to take one step at a time is more than enough. You've got this!

This Inner Workout Book and Card Deck came out of that yearning in me. Wanting to feel loved, accepted, and worthy of love. And, try as I might, something always blocked me – myself! That's why the Self word is repeated in every attribute (card). And that's why there is a hyphen between the attribute and the Self. They are connected and inseparable if you want to truly love yourself and flourish in life.

It doesn't mean you and times in your life will always be Self-Wonderful. In fact, the Self-Woundings are the blessings that come in the form of a wound that, once faced, embraced, and cared for, (dare I say loved and accepted for what it offers), creates the motivational force toward your own ongoing transformation. They are the deep parts of your essence that prompt (and perhaps force) you toward growth and learning more about yourself so you can transform into that amazing, awesome, beautiful, blessed, bold, brave, brilliant, capable, chosen, clever, compassionate, confident, courageous, driven, educated, empowered, fabulous, fantastic, fearless, fierce, forgiving, funny, genuine, grateful, honest, humble, important, incredible, influential, innovative, intelligent, kind, loved, magic, magnificent, motivated, needed, open, passionate, powerful, resilient, resourceful, smart, strong, successful, talented, tenacious, thoughtful, unapologetic, unique, unstoppable, valuable, wanted, wise, worthy, wonderful and more than enough person you were created to be!

You can be all of these as you begin to learn to love yourself wholly in five focus areas, which I call MEPSS: Mentally, Emotionally, Physically, Socially, and Spiritually. Your relationship with yourself is the key to your relationship with everyone and everything else in your life. You are a complete package, and you have all you need at every given moment to be Simply Self-Wonderful!

The Simply Self-Wonderful Inner Workout Book, which can be used in conjunction with *The Simply Self-Wonderful Card Deck*, has found its way to you to meet your deepest yearning for something better. You join a myriad of others who yearn for a better self, a better life, a better world to love with all their hearts and be Simply Self-Wonderful.

What is Simply Self-Wonderful?

Self-Wonderful is the gift of being uniquely YOU that shines with all the superlatives imaginable, effervescing like champagne bubbles from your loving heart and life.

Self-Wonderful is being yourself, knowing yourself, and sharing yourself in order to reveal your real, true self in all the ways and words imaginable and available to you.

In contrast, Self-Wounding is recognizing the pain you drag around like a ball and chain that provokes the healing possibility to free and transform into the gift of promised love.

Self-Wounding is a blessing that comes in the form of a wound, that becomes your responsibility for healing. Once faced, embraced, and cared for, it creates the motivational force towards your own ongoing growth and transformation as the Simply Self-Wonderful YOU!

Together the Self-Wonderfuls and Self-Woundings, make up the perfectly imperfect beloved human and Divine child you are.

What I know to be true about the Simply Self-Wonderful You is:

Your relationship with yourself is the most important relationship you will ever have. It plays a key role in your well-being and the life you want to live. What you do, feel, say, and think of yourself matters. Your abilities, dreams, gifts, interests, skills, and talents matter. YOU matter!

You are a perfectly imperfect beloved child of the Divine Benevolent Mystery of the Universe. Whether or not you consider yourself religious or spiritual, you have a Divine spark or seed of holiness that is an intrinsic part of you that influences you toward love, peace, and harmony. You know this reality and can use whatever word fits best for you Divine/God/Higher Power/Mystery/Source/Universe or something uniquely yours!

You were created to be creative. Creativity is a sacred act of being who you are, finding actions, images, and words for your feelings, instincts, and thoughts by translating your inner life into outward forms to add something worthwhile to the world.

You have a unique set of abilities, gifts, skills, talents, and some important piece of truth to offer the world. These gifts are yours to use generously and wisely in an endless variety of ways, some of which may surprise you (and the world too)!

You create your reality through your actions, emotions, thoughts, and often omissions. This is not just another 'New Age' statement, but one expressed in various philosophical and religious traditions and is now proven by science, especially quantum physics. It's not about fulfilling your own personal desires and having everything you ever wanted, although some people use it that way. The deeper message is one of empowerment, growth, and transformation as you become aware of how your actions, emotions, thoughts, and omissions have consequences based on the choices you make.

You have been wounded and have wounded others in large and small ways. You have suffered from trauma in some form, often many, and must heal so that you can truly flourish in life. Trauma is universal and invisible. It is an emotional response to a perceived event, situation, or threat that leaves you feeling intensely fearful, isolated, overwhelmed, and unsafe (even if you perceived the trauma as peaceful). In fact, everyone experiences trauma differently, and what may feel traumatic to you may not be out of the ordinary for someone else. All of the Self-Woundings and even the Self-Wonderfuls have some link to trauma in your early life.

You are loved more than you will ever know! You are made for love. Love is complicated, and you may never come to full understanding of love. Don't let this prevent you from opening yourself up to experiences of love. Love is deeper and more stable than an emotion. Love is an intention and an action. It is an act of the will to extend yourself for the purpose of your own or another's spiritual growth. Love is a steadfast constant that survives everything. Love is a way of unconditional living and being that heals, motivates, and transforms your life, the people, and the world you love. Love declares: You are Simply Self-Wonderful!

Inspirations for Exploring Simply Self-Wonderful

Personal Empowerment – *The Simply Self-Wonderful Inner Workout Book* and *The Simply Self-Wonderful Card Deck* are means of taking control of your life. By offering your choices and challenges to grow, reach goals, identify what you want from life and take action to achieve all that you dream of, you will have more impact over the world around you and flourish in life.

Spiritual Development – *The Simply Self-Wonderful Inner Workout Book* and *The Simply Self-Wonderful Card Deck* involve the realization that you are not only your body, emotions, and thoughts living in the physical plane of this life, but are also, in reality a soul that must also do spiritual work to maintain your Divine connection and enjoy spiritual maturity as Simply Self-Wonderful!

Have Fun! – Having fun is liberating! It allows you to embody a mixture of connection, flow, and playfulness while being immersed and involved in an activity ultimately intended for pure enjoyment. It is the secret to a healthy, long, and successful life. So, above all else, have fun with your Workout, knowing you are Simply Self-Wonderful!

How to Use This Workout Book

There are no particular 'rules' for using *The Simply Self-Wonderful Inner Workout Book.* It is best used along with *The Simply Self-Wonderful Card Deck,* as this Inner Workout Book expands on the basic information in the Card Deck and gives you many more options for exploring each attribute. In fact, if you only do one exercise a day, it will take you over a year and a half to cover them all once.

Let your intuition and intention for your heart guide you to choose the card attribute that will enhance your day and understanding of yourself. There are 33 Self-Wonderfuls and 32 Self-Woundings. You can choose just one or one Self-Wonderful and one Self-Wounding or try whatever combination of card attributes you sense is most beneficial to you at the moment. And then, within that card attribute or attributes, you can choose the exercise or exercises that attract or challenge you in the moment.

Preparing Yourself

*Choose a time in your day when you can take a few moments for yourself in a safe, comfortable, and welcoming place.
*Clear any distractions or unhealthy energy from the space.
*Choose a card attribute and gaze at it.
*Notice your initial sensations and feelings in your body.
*Read the message.
*Be silent for a few moments to let the message sink in and connect to your deepest inner self but try not to think about it too much.
*Instead, allow the card attribute to begin the healing necessary for your deep healing.
*Choose one or more activities to focus on. Set a timer if you must, or plan time in your day to complete the one you have chosen to focus on.
*Hold yourself accountable in some way for completing the activity.
*Claim this aspect of your Simply Self-Wonderful self and/or offer appreciation for the Self-Wounding blessing that is creating your ongoing transformation.

* Give yourself a hug.
*Continue with your day, knowing you are Simply Self-Wonderful!
*Return to the card at the end of the day and recall and perhaps journal or note the insights, nudge, and ah-ha moments you experienced, reminding you that you are Simply Self-Wonderful!

Structure of the Simply Self-Wonderful Card Deck and Inner Workout Book

There are 2 suits:

Self-Wonderfuls – the many ways you express and reveal the gift of being uniquely you.

Self-Woundings – a blessing that comes in the form of a wound.

As you reflect on each attribute, you will explore the many selves that make up the gifts of being uniquely Self-Wonderful and the Self-Woundings, the blessings that come in the form of a wound that, once faced, embraced, and cared for (dare I say, loved and accepted for what it offers), the motivational force toward your own ongoing transformation as the Simply Self-Wonderful YOU!

Each Card Attribute contains a definition and descriptive message, affirmations, quotes, 5 MEPSS activities, and a corresponding mandala to color.

Definition – defines a Self-Wonderful or a Self-Wounding.

Descriptive Message – goes deeper and explores the particular attribute of the Self.

Affirmations – phrases to say repeatedly to yourself with confidence and conviction that embody who you want to become, help you think in ways that make your life better, and prompt new desired actions and behaviors. To make them more powerful:
- Say them out loud 3 times, several times a day, as you get ready for the day. Look in the mirror as you sit at a stoplight and repeat them when waiting in line or before falling asleep. Or pair them with self-care activities or exercise.
- Say them with as much confidence, conviction, emotion, and motivation as possible.
- Visualize what you are affirming as having already happened.
- Write them out using your own handwriting, decorate them, put them in a visible place, or tuck one in your lunchbox, purse, wallet, or other place where it can surprise you daily.

Quotes – chosen for the succinct expression of the concept. Use them for action, inspiration, motivation, and self-coaching, and enjoy their well-expressed wisdom.

MEPSS Activities – enhance your relationship with your Simply Self-Wonderful Self in 5 focus areas:
M – stands for your **mental** center of intelligence and often challenges your beliefs, stories, and thoughts.
E – stands for your **emotional** center of intelligence and looks at how you can use your emotions and feelings more effectively in your life.
P – stands for **physical** or your body intelligence and often asks you to reflect on your physical body as the only vehicle you have to live your life from in this life.
S – (the **first** one) stands for **social** and looks at the aspects and actions in your relationships.
S – (the **final** one) stands for **spiritual** and catalyzes your Divine connection through your spirit and soul.

Resources – Some of the activities have an asterisk * to point you to more information found here.

A **mandala** – the activity that started it all, *The Simply Self-Wonderful Inner Workout Book* contains a corresponding mandala to color, designed by Tanya Back to reveal all the subtleties of the various definitions. Mandalas are a continuous circular shape that balances energy in the body, calms the mind, and promotes healing of the body.

Focusing on and coloring a mandala lets the Universe know you are placing your desire and intention on healing and wholeness. The simple act of coloring helps you work through the outer chaos and confusion in your life and get in touch and be present with your inner being for greater acceptance, knowledge, love, and understanding of yourself. So, make time to release your creativity, return to your inner child, and grab your crayons, colored pencils, or markers. Fill it in all at once or start with one characteristic that fascinates you and do a bit at a time.

And if you don't want to color in the workout book itself, it is okay to copy the page for yourself as long as the copyright information shows. If you want to use it for a group exercise, you will need permission from the author and publisher.

A Yearly Practice and More

With 65 cards, each with multiple affirmations, quotes, MEPSS exercises, and a mandala to color, there are over 500 activities to choose from. This means you have over a year and a half of creative, inspirational, and transformational activities to choose from to create and grow the Simply Self-Wonderful YOU!

Get ready to begin this perpetual journey of discovery to deeper love, growth, and transformation of the Simply Self-Wonderful YOU

Self-Wonderful

Self-Wonderful is the gift of being uniquely YOU that shines with all the superlatives imaginable, effervescing like champagne bubbles from your loving heart and life.

Self-Wonderful is being yourself, knowing yourself, and sharing yourself to reveal your real, true self in all the ways and words that describe the amazing, awesome, beautiful, blessed, bold, brave, brilliant, capable, chosen, clever, compassionate, confident, courageous, driven, educated, empowered, fabulous, fantastic, fearless, fierce, forgiving, funny, genuine, grateful, honest, humble, important, incredible, influential, innovative, intelligent, kind, loved, magic, magnificent, motivated, needed, open, passionate, powerful, resilient, resourceful, smart, strong, successful, talented, tenacious, thoughtful, unapologetic, unique, unstoppable, valuable, wanted, wise, worthy, wonderful – more than enough YOU!

Your relationship with yourself is the most important relationship you will ever have. It plays a key role in your well-being and the life you want to live. What you do, feel, say, and think of yourself matters. Your abilities, dreams, gifts, interests, skills, and talents matter. YOU matter.

You must put yourself first. You have the right to make decisions and take the time to take care of yourself in a way that gives you the authority, autonomy, and power to live the life you want, with no exceptions or excuses. You have the right to exist exactly as you are.

Self-Wonderful is about accepting and honoring your humanness and the 'human-mess' that sometimes happens when you are bumping up against your limitations as you do the best you can, given your own unique history, environment, genetic capabilities, choices, and a myriad of variables you encounter each day.

Your level of commitment to yourself determines your state of Self-Wonderful and is not based on parental evaluation, societal expectations, or any other tendency to devalue your worth as a perfectly imperfect, beloved child of the Divine, living a spiritual life in a human body on earth at this time – your time, a time of growth and enrichment to live fully into who you were created to be.

There is no arrival. You already are Self-Wonderful, yet it's also an ongoing journey to be better and get more of what you want for yourself in this lifetime. So be the gift of being uniquely YOU that shines with all the superlatives imaginable, effervescing like champagne bubbles from your loving heart and life. You are Simply Self-Wonderful!

I am Simply Self-Wonderful.
I am a wonderful expression of the Divine.
I am the only version of myself to ever exist in the universe.

"By being yourself, you put something wonderful in the world that was not there before." –Edwin Elliot

"Has anyone ever told you how wonderful you are? Just in case they haven't, you deserve to know… the world is a brighter place because you are in it. You are wonderful." –SimpLee Serene

"Wake up. Be wonderful. Repeat." –Adrienne Posey

MEPSS Activities

Mental – Make a bucket list of 10 things you would dare to do to be your true self. What beliefs, excuses, hesitations, or reasons have stopped you? Imagine the wonderful life you will have after you have done each one and write a word or phrase of encouragement that includes a first action step for 2 of them. Ask another person to hold you accountable. Give yourself 1 week to do it. If you don't do it, the other person must give you a dare to do it as well.

Emotional – You are already making something wonderful of yourself. I promise. Create an acrostic* beginning with each letter of the word WONDERFUL. Write a word or phrase for each of the letters with something wonderful about yourself.

Physical – Starting with your head, move down through each of your body parts, both those inside and outside, and tell each part, 'You are wonderfully made and make me wonderful.' Offer some form of appreciation to each. Do this regularly until it becomes natural.

Social – From the list of words in the encouragement section describing all the qualities that might make up you, choose 15 words and add examples from your life when you displayed these to the world and were recognized for it, even if only by yourself. And if there are more, by all means, claim those too!

Spiritual – Wonder is the feeling of surprise mingled with admiration caused by something beautiful, unexpected, unfamiliar, or inexplicable. Wonder begins in the senses, comes alive in the imagination, and flourishes in adoration of the sacred. Spend 10 minutes being curious about the grand adventure of your life. Start by saying 'I wonder…' and see what arises, and what comes next, and next, and so forth. Notice where your wonder takes you. What happens next? Be it. Create it. Do it. Say it. See it. Try it!

Self-Acceptance

Self-Acceptance is the gift of a big A-OK that welcomes all parts of you unconditionally.

Self-Acceptance is the lifelong process of learning to love yourself inside and out. It's about being comfortable with who you are in the moment and accepting that everything about you is meant to enhance your understanding of yourself as uniquely you! It's appreciating what makes you unique and letting go of the things you can't change.

It also means letting go of whom you and others think and say you're supposed to be, offering forgiveness, and embracing who you are without thoughts of judgment, comparison with others, or any other conditions, exceptions, or qualifications. There is nothing to "fix"; you are acceptable unconditionally just as you are.

When parents and others, including unspoken and unrealistic standards of society, accept you only conditionally, you learn that your acceptance depends on how you act. Your behavior isn't acceptable to them, and you learn to regard yourself as faulty and inferior and internalize feelings of rejection. This leads to the Self-Wounding of Self-Criticism, where you see yourself as inadequate and operate from a place of less than.

Practicing Self-Acceptance helps you understand that you are not to blame for anything—your looks, your intelligence, your emotions, or your feelings—and you are already OK without qualifications. That's what grace is! There is nothing you have to do or be other than yourself. It's not that you ignore or deny your frailties or strengths; it's that you can see them as irrelevant to your acceptance of yourself. And you always have the choice to do something about them if you decide to.

Being willing to confront what you find so difficult to accept about yourself determines your level of happiness. Telling yourself that you've done the best you could is a great place to start. Re-examining feelings of shame, guilt, criticism, and judgment through the lens of another Self-Wonderful, Self-Compassion, can help you learn to like yourself more and accept your birthright of love and respect. Offering forgiveness also helps you let go of the untruths that helped you cope in the moment. In the end, you'll realize that there's nothing to forgive and that's it's more about making peace with the parts of yourself that, until now, have been shunned, denied, or put down.

When you learn to validate your own essential "OK-ness" and affirm who you are, with your strengths and weaknesses, the more Self-Acceptance you will have in your life and the more you will be able to love and appreciate yourself over your lifetime. The more Self-Acceptance you have, the more positive you will become, and the more happiness you will allow yourself to accept, receive, enjoy, and offer to others.

Self-Acceptance makes it possible to accept and love yourself and still be committed to a lifetime of personal growth. Accepting yourself as you are today can still offer motivation to experiment, make changes, and try on some new qualities or behaviors that will make you a more effective and fulfilled person.

But Self-Acceptance isn't tied to these changes! It's about your personal preferences. It's up to you to decide if you want or need to make changes. Remember, you don't have to do anything to secure your Self-Acceptance. You are A-OK! You are accepted! Period!

I love and accept myself just the way I am.

I love and believe in the person that lives in my body and carries me through the day.

My uniqueness is my blessing.

"Self-acceptance is perhaps the best gift you can give yourself." *–Anonymous*

"Self-acceptance is my refusal to be in an adversarial relationship with myself." –Nathaniel Branden

"What self-acceptance does is open up more possibilities of succeeding because you aren't fighting yourself along the way." –Shannon Ables

MEPSS Activities

Mental – Making mental comparisons and rating yourself are defense mechanisms. Carry a stack of Post-it notes and a pen with you for one day. Write down all the ratings you give yourself. Then create a simple ritual to void those ratings by offering a self-accepting, affirming counter-message to yourself for each one.

Emotional – When you accept yourself, you are free from the burden of needing acceptance from another. Make a list of 10 ways you have tried to get others to love and accept you. Now, be kind and accepting of yourself by spending quality time with yourself without any monetary cost. (Take a bubble bath, go for a walk in nature, etc.) Enjoy having fun, be creative, and nurture yourself.

Physical – Go ahead. Get it over with. Focus on all those body parts that don't meet your standards. Then celebrate their uniqueness and accept them as they are.

Social – Get out into the world! Volunteer or try a new extracurricular activity to learn more about yourself, what you enjoy, and what you are good at. Let other people praise you and accept it without offering anything other than an expression of gratitude or thanks.

Spiritual – Self-Acceptance is akin to grace*. "Grace is something you can never get but can only be given… There's nothing *you* have to do. There's nothing you *have* to do. There's nothing you have to *do*… There's only one catch. Like any other gift, the gift of grace can only be yours only if you reach out and take it. Maybe being able to reach out and take it is a gift too." Frederick Buechner*

Practice GRACE with yourself

G – Gift – List five occasions where you were a unique gift to others. For each one, write how they benefited from what you uniquely had to offer. Make a symbol that summarizes these gifts and gift it back to yourself by placing it where you will see it several times a day.

R – Respect – List five qualities that need more of your respect. Honor them with an inner bow of appreciation, saying you are 'A-OK' regularly, and notice what shifts inside you.

A – Accept – List five things you can't change about yourself. Accept each of them as they are by naming the ways they have contributed to your growth and understanding of yourself.

C – Celebrate – List five things that make you unique. Celebrate each one with a simple activity, gesture, or small token of appreciation.

E – Embody – List five ways you can practice Self-Acceptance. Start doing one today.

A-OK
Self Acceptance
Self Acceptance
Self Acceptance
Self Acceptance

Self-Actualization

Self-Actualization is the gift of owning the state of your life fully and joyfully expressing the magnificence that is YOU.

"Self-actualization is the oxygen for the soul." –Brian Johnson

"In life, you don't get instant satisfaction. In life, you get to slog. You work. You grow. You take the long view. You fill the void with self-actualization." –Amy Dickinson

*"Musicians must make music, artists must paint, poets must write if they are to be ultimately at peace with themselves. What human beings can be, they must be. They must be true to their own nature. This need we may call self-actualization." –Abraham Maslow**

Self-Actualization is the highest level of self-growth. It is a place of authenticity you can reach when you act in congruence with your authentic self and do not limit yourself to self-imposed thoughts or images. Self-Actualization is a personal goal you strive for by pursuing the excellence and enjoyment of your full potential. It can be viewed as a component of well-being and taps into your desire to reach your full creative, intellectual, and social potential. It is not about making the most money, achieving the highest status possible, having things always go smoothly, or reaching perfection (which is impossible anyway!). You can become self-actualized and still face difficulties in life. In fact, once you are clear that Self-Actualization is about recognizing your limits in addition to focusing on your unique strengths, it can open wide the door of possibility in your own life.

Self-Actualization is about achieving anything that sparks your passion. It is a constant work in process. There is really no end. And as you continue to strive toward self-actualization, you will begin to have a sense of reality and truth and focus on things that are bigger than yourself. You are in touch with actual possibilities to engage in or not. You will feel more comfortable with the unknown and don't mind not knowing what the future holds for you. You live more spontaneously and naturally and enjoy what happens in the moment. You enjoy peak experiences and have a sense of feeling connected to the larger universe where your heart opens, and a deeper meaning becomes clear. You look at things more creatively and think differently than other people do. You live more independently and are not swayed by the opinions and social feedback of others. You have compassion, kindness, and acceptance both for yourself and for others. You have meaningful, long-lasting relationships rather than casual friendships with many people. You have a sense of justice and work to prevent injustice and unethical behavior. You have a good-natured sense of humor and can laugh at yourself when you make mistakes and help others see the humor in challenging situations. You appreciate each moment and know that you are never going to stay completely the same.

Self-Actualization fills your life with purpose and authenticity as you strive to grow, get comfortable with, and care for yourself as well as show love and concern for others. Your Self-Actualization is unique to you. You own your life fully and joyfully, expressing the magnificence that is YOU. That's part of what makes it so Simply Self-Wonderful.

I have the power to live my dreams and manifest my highest potential.

I stand in all that I am and live from my authentically true self.

Am I good enough? Yes, I am. (an affirmation from former First Lady Michelle Obama)

MEPSS Activities

Mental – Practicing acceptance by learning to accept what comes as it comes can help you achieve Self-Actualization. The next time a situation doesn't turn out the way you wished it would, say this simple yet mind-changing mantra '*This is the gift of what is here now. I accept and embrace it and seek the wisdom in this moment.*'

Emotional – Get comfortable with your own company by giving yourself some 'me-time.' Choose a time today to do something to reconnect with yourself in a simple, calm, peaceful way. Celebrate this nurturing demonstration of your relationship with yourself by journaling about a new discovery you had about yourself.

Physical – Stop and smell some flowers today. Take a deep breath in and a deep breath out, sending oxygen into your body and releasing carbon dioxide on the exhale. Appreciate the moment as if it was totally new to you.

Social – Self-Actualized people have deep compassion for others and the world. Choose a group of people who have very different life experiences than you by reading or listening to media produced by those from a different background. Then agree to do one small thing to celebrate, encourage, or support them that you would want to be done to yourself if given the same opportunity.

Spiritual – Have a conversation about what you have mastered along the way to Self-Actualization with the Divine/God/Higher Power/Mystery/Source/Universe*. You can use a different voice, style of handwriting, non-dominant handwriting*, or any other thing to distinguish between you and the Divine*. Have fun!!!!

Self Actualization
You You You You You You You You

Self-Appreciation

Self-Appreciation is the gift of gratitude you offer yourself by bowing to honor your true value and worth.

Self-Appreciation is about accepting your uniqueness with kindness and gratitude. You say, 'Thank you' to yourself for everything you have done but have taken for granted. Self-Appreciation recognizes the value within you, who you are, and what you do. It's not about becoming someone different but celebrating who you already are. It is about consciously acknowledging all the strengths within you without the need to compare yourself to others. It's about taking time to appreciate all the good things you do for yourself, others, and the larger world. You operate from a sense of true humility as you acknowledge your beliefs, trust your instincts, and accept all parts of yourself, including those parts that you might label as weaknesses.

Sometimes it's hard to appreciate yourself, and it may even make you uncomfortable at first. You've learned from others who have had a hard time themselves with Self-Appreciation that it's so much easier to cut yourself down. You have learned to focus on what you see as 'wrong' about yourself, or what disappoints you, or what has let you down previously rather than face another doing the same to you.

Self-Appreciation is the foundation of a happy and fulfilling life. Self-Appreciation develops a sense of peace within yourself. You allow yourself to acknowledge that all people have strengths and weaknesses. Self-Appreciation offers the foundation to separate how you perceive yourself and how your 'imaginary audience' sees you. You no longer need to succumb to external pressure to be someone else. You have no need to try to be 'different.' You have no need to blame yourself for making mistakes, forgetting to do things, or acting unaware. Instead, you allow yourself to revel in all your goodness without feeling arrogant or overconfident. You become the best version of yourself.

Self-Appreciation doesn't mean living in a self-centered world. It doesn't mean being naïve or overly optimistic. It offers you a healthy, balanced perspective of yourself, and because of this, you can stand in yourself and have a healthy, balanced perspective of others. You appreciate that everyone has goodness in them as part of who they intrinsically are. When you appreciate yourself, then it's easier to appreciate others.

Self-Appreciation allows you to turn the kindness you give to others toward yourself.

When you treat yourself with the same kindness you treat your friends, you will have the support and care required to truly thrive in life. You learn that it no longer matters whether or not anyone else appreciates you. Instead, others' approval and appreciation become the opportunity to affirm your own inner values and be able to align yourself to them in a more appreciative way, offering yourself the gift of gratitude by bowing to honor your true value and worth.

I love and fully appreciate my blessed uniqueness.

My appreciation of myself is infinite and limitless.

I appreciate all opportunities to grow my true self.

"When was the last time you thanked you for always being there for you? Self-appreciation soothes an aching soul."
–Iyanla Vanzant

"Self-appreciation is a sign of maturity, seeking appreciation is a sign of immaturity." –Sivaprakash Sidhu

"The less approval I get, the more chances I have to develop a relationship with my inner sense of approval. Thankless environments are actually useful for this. They help me discover my own thankfulness and my own self-appreciation." –Vironika Tugaleva

MEPSS Activities

Mental – Be grateful for your mind! Being able to think, remember, and solve problems makes life easier and is one of the things that we don't often even think about. Solve a puzzle today – a crossword, a 100-piece jigsaw, the daily Wordle, Brain Teaser, or any other favorite of yours. Offer thanks to your Mind every time you have an answer or put in a puzzle piece.

Emotional – Take some time today to appreciate yourself. List 10 good things you do for yourself, 10 good things you do for other people, and 10 good things you do for the world. Of course, you can always expand it to 25 or 50 if you're on a roll!!! Then give yourself a bow of gratitude for each and everything on the list!

Physical – Find a fun anatomy book and go through it to appreciate each body part, the systems, and processes that all work together to keep you alive and healthy. Learn 5 fun facts and share them in a creative way. Bonus: Learn the difference between the Western and Eastern Medical models* and see what each can offer for your health concerns.

Social – Appreciate your ability to listen to others, to laugh, to play, to be of service, and choose one thing you can offer back to the world by volunteering your time and resources to a cause that you appreciate.

Spiritual – When we are in a state of appreciation, we transmit some of the highest and most spiritual energy vibrations possible. Louise L. Hay* says, *'The more grateful you are, the more you have to be grateful for.'* Be easily impressed. Appreciate the miracle of life itself and your living presence on this earth right now.

SELF-APPRECIATION

Self-Assurance

Self-Assurance is the gift of standing tall with certainty in the face of uncertainty.

Self-Assurance is a sense of certainty in yourself no matter what others say about you or whatever difficult situations you encounter. You can confront whatever life throws at you because you are sure of your ability to overcome it. Self-Assurance comes from being deeply rooted in your identity, potential, and values. It's a belief in yourself that makes you sure of who you are. You have a firm conviction, grasp, and knowledge of your character and capabilities and feel confident about yourself.

Self-Assurance relies on how you evaluate yourself, which, of course, is subjective and must be developed. If you want to experience greater Self-Assurance, you must face your fears. Fear is a natural part of being human; its job is to warn you of impending danger. Fear is most helpful when there is physical danger, but there are other kinds of fear, such as fear of rejection, failure, judgment, inadequacy, loneliness, or being emotionally hurt, which aren't resolved as easily as just fleeing the danger. You must work with these kinds of fears in a different way. Instead of seeing fear as something to overcome or conquer, approach it with curiosity, knowing that something will be revealed and notice where it might be asking you to start understanding the patterns and situations where it appears. Use fear as your ally to grow your Self-Assurance, as it empowers you to become more sure of yourself and your abilities.

Self-Assurance happens when you've found your purpose for living and live your life with intention to maximize your full potential. Standing in your Self-Assurance makes it easier to voice your opinions, stand up for yourself in relationships, and create the opportunities you desire for your future. There is a sense of trust in your own ability to deal with failure, knowing that failure is crucial to your success. You can accept mistakes as necessary parts of the learning process.

Cultivating Self-Assurance involves other Self-Wonderfuls such as Self-Confidence and Self-Esteem so that you can feel sure of yourself in a calm, cool, and collected way. Self-Assurance brings the gift of standing tall in your uniqueness to the world.

I stand tall in who I am.

I face uncertainty with certainty.

I am self-assured, comfortable, and confident in who I am.

"Self-assurance doesn't come from looking perfect and having a great title, but from accepting yourself with all your mistakes and eccentricities." –Cecelie Berry

"We can enjoy a self-assurance that doesn't depend on the state of things outside ourselves, be it downturns or booms or whatever." –Desmond Tutu

"The power of a bold idea uttered publicly in defiance of dominant opinion cannot be easily measured. Those special people who speak out in such a way as to shake up not only the self-assurance of their enemies, but the complacency of their friends, are precious catalysts for change." –Howard Zinn

MEPSS Activities

Mental – Picture yourself in a situation that has recently kept your mind going in circles. Have fun visualizing yourself standing tall on the stack of strengths you already have. Claim them! Now, mentally rehearse the words you would say. Include what you would say if you were interrupted before you could get it all out. Visualize possible actions and see yourself making it happen easily and effectively. Find a picture that reminds you of your Self-Assurance and have it close by when you feel uncertain about yourself.

Emotional – Embrace your fears by making a list of fears that hold you back from Self-Assurance. Be curious with one of them by having a back-and-forth inner conversation using nondominant handwriting*. With your dominant hand, write what you are feeling. If you can't express it in words, then draw a picture or just scribble, or make sounds. Then, use your nondominant hand to draw, scribble, or utter a sound. Continue back and forth until you gain some new insight into your fear. Celebrate that insight in a simple way and stand in this new revelation about yourself. Later, you can get curious with another fear on your list.

Physical – There is nothing that says Self-Assurance like proper posture*! Stand tall with your feet aligned with your hipbones, not too narrow or too wide. Keep your chin up so that your eyes are focused straight ahead, not down at the floor. Align your shoulders with your hips and keep them soft and wide, open, and sure. Keep your chest focused outward, not rounded, or hunched, in a way that invites life and breath into your heart and lungs. Keep your spine slightly stretched upward so that it straightens naturally without feeling stiff and immovable. Imagine a balloon string tethered to the top of your head that keeps you lifted while staying grounded in the downward force of gravity. Feel and remember the buoyancy this creates as your body is balanced, aligned, supported, and working in harmony with every other part.

Social – Who is your personal 'Shero'? Is there someone you admire for their Self-Assurance and certainty in uncertain situations? It can be someone you know personally, a fictional character in a book or movie, or a celebrity you admire. Make a list of the qualities that point to their Self-Assurance, then choose one to emulate. When you successfully integrate it, add more to build your belief in yourself.

Spiritual – One of the simplest ways to feel Self-Assurance is to know what purpose moves you through life with intention. This is not an easy undertaking, but it can become clearer by listening to the voice within. Pause right now, take a deep breath in and out. Allow your body, mind, and spirit to become present to that quiet voice, that warm glow or tingle of excitement that evokes joy in you. What do you sense? What would being and doing more of that offer you? Take a small first step to direct you closer to your joy and living your life with purpose and intention.

Self-
Assurance

Self-Awareness

Self-Awareness is the gift of a deeply internal, heart knowing of yourself in each moment.

Self-Awareness means that you are mindful of who you are, how you treat yourself and others, how you deal with challenges, and how you interact with your environment. When you can do this, you are more likely to live a happier, healthier, and more fulfilling life because you have done the work necessary to arrive at a place of choice and full alignment with your true self.

Self-Awareness allows you to change the relationship to the thoughts in your mind and choose to separate from the voices in your head that no longer serve you, changing them into ones that support your best overall functioning. It also means that you can be present with your emotions and can choose how to use them for the best outcome. Self-Awareness also allows you to notice your body language and nervous system response. Self-Awareness also helps you identify the false identity and false thinking your mind projects so you can see yourself differently as you look inward and discover your true self.

Self-Awareness is a subtle state of perception that occurs in the gap between having a thought or an emotion and being able to choose how you will respond. It is that quick and will flee just as quickly if you don't practice catching it and acting on it. That means you can actually observe your thinking and emotions, analyze them quickly, see the limitations and possibilities, be skeptical or accepting, and consider alternate perspectives and options all in a matter of seconds.

Self-Awareness gives you the ability to deal with your thoughts, emotions, beliefs, and behaviors in life-affirming ways. You know who you are deep inside and use each day to live toward your dreams, goals, and true purpose in life. You treat others well because you can deal effectively with other people's thinking, emotions, beliefs, and behaviors because you are genuinely happy with yourself. You live proactively rather than reactively and feel more at peace inside. You offer yourself the gift of a deeply internal, heart-knowing of yourself in each moment.

I know myself.

I am aware of who I am and make choices to support my true self.

I am conscious and aware of myself in the present moment.

"Self-awareness is the ability to take an honest look at your life without any attachment to it being right or wrong, good or bad." –Debbie Ford

'Wisdom tends to grow in proportion to self-awareness of one's ignorance.' –Anthony de Mello

"Without self-awareness, we are as babies in the cradles." –Virginia Woolf

MEPSS Activities

Mental – Choose a way to practice mindfulness* by mindful walking, listening, or eating. Pay attention to your inner state as it arises. Note, without becoming attached to, your thoughts, emotions, and commentary as they arise and allow them to pass like clouds in the moment. Note which ones are repetitive and tend to have harmful effects.

Emotional – Use a journal to process your emotions through writing or drawing. Notice what themes, thoughts, and beliefs are attached to your emotions. Which ones arise again and again? Then ask yourself – What do I want? What values show up? What works for me? You can also ask the opposite questions – What don't I want? What's not important to me? What doesn't work for me? However, reframing things in the positive is always better as your brain hears the 'nots' and doesn't cancel them out.

Physical – Choose a physical activity or sport that you engage in regularly. Now, gain a different perspective by observing what others do either in person, via television, or in an online video. Observe their emotions and body language without judging or evaluating. Then observe your emotions and body language as it responded to watching the other person. What did you learn about yourself? What might you do differently next time to improve your practice?

Social – Practice listening to another person by asking a family member or friend what they think about you. Have them describe you and see what rings true with you and what surprises you. Carefully consider what they say and think as you reflect or journal afterward and become more self-aware.

Spiritual – Create a quiet and comfortable space for you to connect with yourself daily at a regular time if possible. Turn off all tech devices that might distract you. Make the space inviting by having a lit candle or small visual object to hold or focus on. Ask a question you'd like to explore, then allow the thoughts, bodily sensations, and nonverbal intuitive hits to come. There may not be an immediate answer at the moment, or even a complete sentence, so don't discount anything that arises; just accept what comes. If you can, put whatever comes figuratively and intentionally under your pillow and sleep on it. Notice what arises in the morning. Waking from sleep often brings new insights and clarity. Each time you do this, your inner energies will wake up, work miracles, and offer more Self-Awareness.

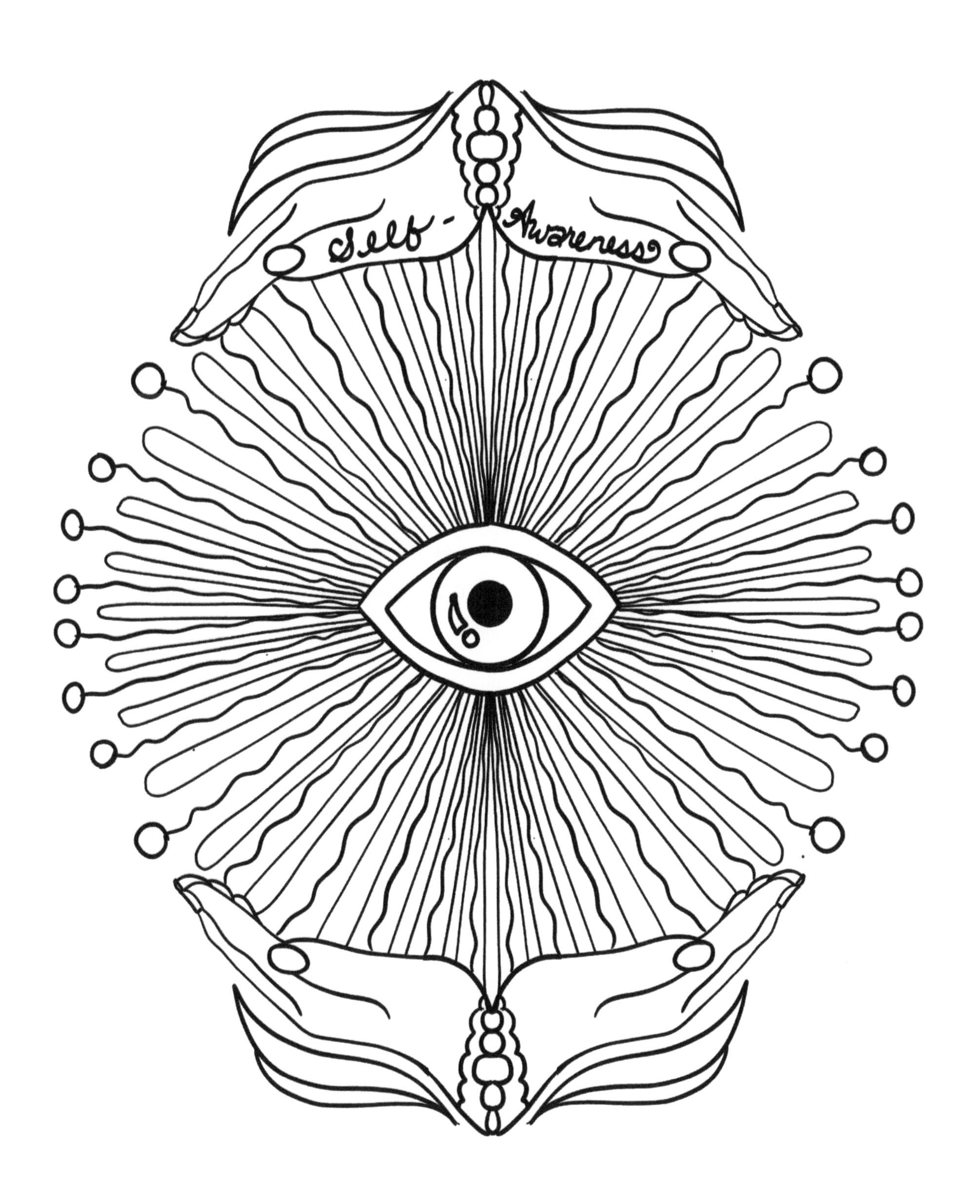
Self-Awareness

Self-Care

Self-Care is the deliberate gift you give yourself religiously to renew your zest for life.

Instead of asking, 'Do I take care of myself?' ask yourself, 'In what ways do I take care of myself?' That's a bit trickier, yet, it can make all the difference.

Self-Care is any way of tending to yourself that pays attention to you, not in a Selfish or narcissistic way as some might think, but in a way that ensures you are being cared for by yourself. It is something that refuels you rather than takes energy from you. It's not only done in consideration of your needs but is more about knowing what you need to take care of your whole self and others. For if you don't take good care of yourself, you won't be able to give to your loved ones in the ways they need it most.

Self-Care is the key to living a balanced life, not in terms of equal and equal but rather functionally working together efficiently as a whole. It means that you know who you are and your own limits. It means you are the one in the driver's seat of your health and well-being and know when to accelerate and when to put on the brakes. As you practice Self-Care, you will find your own rhythm and routine. You will work it into your schedule and stick to it. And you must see it as Self-Care, or you will discard it to your own detriment. Self-Care goes a long way in managing the stress life brings and toward living your best and healthiest life.

There are as many Self-Care practices as there are people, and only you know what will be just right for you. Be creative! Whether they are small (like intentionally taking a breath in and out every now and then), or big (an all-day splurge), make sure they are fun, include laughter and play, as well as the discipline of eating, exercising, and sleeping the right amounts for you. They may also include other people since our relationships often bring us so much love and joy! True Self-Care has a quality of reverence for being alive, deepens your experience of living life, and, done religiously, renews your zest for life. You are worth it, after all!!!!

I give myself the Self-Care and attention I need.

I give myself permission to do what is right for me.

I breathe in and out with intention and offer myself Self-Care with every breath.

"Self-care is never a selfish act – it is simply good stewardship of the only gift I have, the gift I was put on earth to offer to others." –Parker Palmer

"Self-care is giving the world the best of you, instead of what's left of you." –Katie Reed

"Self-care is how you take your power back." –Lalah Delia

MEPSS Activities

Mental – Give your mind a break! Send that thinking brain on a 'play date' while you take time to relax, go blank, imagine, or meditate for a few minutes many times throughout your day. Create a 'structure' that reminds you to pause.

Emotional – Decompressing after work or clearing the clutter of 'Other People's Energy'* after a stressful day is important. Take time to recreate your boundaries, giving people back their energy and taking back your own.

Physical – Get to know your body's needs* and limits by paying attention to your energy levels throughout the day and the activities associated with them. Are you getting enough or too much food, exercise, or sleep? Are you eating healthy food or snacking on empty calories and sugar? Are you working too many hours or too hard?

Commit to shifting in one area in small and gradual increments.

Social – Ask yourself, Is there anything I can choose to do or change in my work or school situation to make it less stressful, more fun, and easier to deal with?

Spiritual – Put yourself at the top of your 'to-do list' every single day. Take time to love yourself! Appreciate your unique one and only you! Dance, sing, listen to your favorite music; do something creative that makes you feel fully alive and grateful to be here!

SELF-CARE
SELF-CARE
SELF-CARE
SELF-CARE

Self-Celebration

Self-Celebration is the gift of throwing confetti at any time just because you are you.

Self-Celebration is taking some time out for a little fun and self-congratulations and celebrating publicly or privately in big and small ways, appreciating who you are for any reason you choose. Self-Celebration is about bringing some joy into your life by accepting, encouraging, and empowering yourself in the moment, not your past self and not your future self, but who you are right now. It's honoring your efforts and triumphs and praising your resilience for having made it through hard times too.

Self-Celebration is not about bragging, proving you are better than others, loudly proclaiming how amazing you are, trying to prove your worth to someone, or being mean or arrogant. It is not an excuse to falsely celebrate, become inebriated, or use addictive substances to feel better about yourself in the moment. It is also not an excuse to proclaim that you have arrived and don't need to try to do anything more.

Self-Celebration reminds you to take a moment every day and savor it. When you take time to do so, you are accepting and learning to love all parts of the story of your life and who you are, the ones that are easy to love and those that are hard to like and accept. You become proud of who you are and what you have achieved and accomplished. Your confidence in yourself increases and attracts more beneficial energy into your life. When you take time to acknowledge the actions you are taking toward your goals, you strengthen these actions. Taking a moment in Self-Celebration will remind you to enjoy your life journey and to be grateful for all the gifts you have gained—all the highs and lows, ups and downs, and big and small occurrences that make you, you.

Self-Celebration can shift your entire perspective on life. It can help you step into your power, become more productive, gain clarity about what you want in life, and accept all parts of you. It's a support tool you can use for any changes you want to make. Self-Celebration helps you work out what you love to do and do it more. It's a secret superpower that is always within you, one that you can use to cheer yourself on when the going is easy and in more challenging times.

Self-Celebration increases other Self-Wonderfuls and decreases Self-Criticism and other Self-Woundings. So, grab a handful of confetti, toss it in the air, and shout a loud woo-hoo to you!!!

I celebrate my uniquely wonderful self.

I am the best me there is.

I celebrate my gifts and use them to reach my goals.

'The more self-celebration and self-praise in your life, the more there is in life to celebrate.' –Oprah Winfrey

"Celebrate yourself. Follow your passions and eccentricities because they are yours alone. You are unique! If everyone did that, I'm pretty sure there would be world peace." –Kandyse McClure

"When you celebrate yourself, every day is a festival." –Unknown

MEPSS Activities

Mental – Write a letter of appreciation to yourself and highlight all the courageous things you have done to find your way to where you are now. Then put it in an envelope with your address, stamp it, and send it to yourself so you can read it again and again when you receive it.

Emotional – Practice being kind and loving to yourself by starting a weekly pampering ritual to celebrate yourself. It may be a hot bubble bath, watching a favorite movie or show, reading a magazine or book, looking through photo albums, or just giving yourself time to do nothing or whatever you feel like doing in the moment. During that time, be sure to give yourself plenty of self-loving hugs!

Physical – This one is easy! Celebrate yourself with a new picture of yourself. It could be artsy, bold, colorful, formal, contemplative, or black and white. Make sure it is celebratory and includes you with a big smile! You will be glad later that you've documented your Self-Celebration moment!

Social – Have a Self-Celebration gathering with a few friends. Make it a true celebration with food, fun, and festivities. At some point during your time together, go around the group and celebrate each person's unique eccentricities, quirkiness, passions, and strengths. See how these connect, encourage, and propel you to bigger and better things. Then decide as a group to do one thing together for the greater good and peace in the world.

Spiritual – Make a small altar that contains cards, figures, items from nature, pictures, trinkets, and other representations of challenges, obstacles, and struggles that you have dealt with and overcome on the way to becoming who you are today. If you believe you have been guided and assisted by physical or metaphysical helpers, include them in your altar. Spend time here each day offering thanks for the guidance and assistance you have received and for all you have overcome and embraced to become uniquely you.

Self Celebration

Self-Compassion

Self-Compassion is the gift of a warm, caring hug you can give yourself to help cope with anything that comes your way.

Self-Compassion accepts the human condition of imperfection and affirms that you are acceptable, worthy, and valued as a human being who shares the common trait with all other humans, past, present, and future. The more your heart is open to this reality instead of fighting against it or denying it, the more you will feel compassion for yourself and a sense of common humanity with every human experiencing life on this planet.

Self-Compassion allows you to face your struggles, big and small, internal and external, with a sense that you are rooting for yourself as part of a larger team, knowing you have inherent value while learning to dismiss that critical inner voice, address the things you can change, and establish a healthy and authentic sense of self.

Self-Compassion is caring for your inner experience of disappointment, frustration, failure, and suffering with spaciousness, being gentle and caring with yourself. It allows you to accept and just be with any difficult experience in each moment, instead of getting angry about it, trying to fix it, make it go away, get over it, or hide it in the recesses of your suffering and shame.

When you act with kindness and acknowledge your failures and misdeeds rather than Self-Judgment, it shifts your brain out of the negativity bias and allows for a more open, self-nurturing frame of mind. The result is resilience, being able to deal with and recover from stressors in life and rise above them, grow stronger and more reliable. It brings many benefits, including agreeableness, conscientiousness, curiosity, happiness, inquisitiveness, optimism, personal initiative, positivity, wisdom, and even extroversion!

Self-Compassion benefits your psychological well-being more than another Self-Wonderful, Self-Esteem. It offers greater emotional resilience, a more accurate assessment of who you are, and strengthens personal accountability as you act with kindness. Self-Compassion is the antidote for many Self-Woundings and is one of the most powerful sources of coping and resilience available to you. Self-Compassion is not selfishness or focusing on yourself in a narcissistic Self-Wounding way but keeps you equal with others, no better, no worse. You meet your needs in ways you know you can by offering the gift of a warm, caring hug you can give yourself to help cope with anything that comes your way.

I offer myself compassion and tenderness, showing kindness to myself.

I let go of my inner critical voice and embrace my humanness and humanmess.

Self-compassion heals, nourishes, and reconnects all parts of me to love.

*"I found in my research that the biggest reason people aren't more self-compassionate is that they are afraid they'll become self-indulgent. They believe self-criticism is what keeps them in line. Most people have gotten it wrong because our culture says being hard on yourself is the way to be." –Kristen Neff**

*"Self-compassion is key because when we're able to be gentle with ourselves in the midst of shame, we're more likely to reach out, connect, and experience empathy." –Brene Brown**

*"An important aspect of self-compassion is to be able to emphatically hold both parts of ourselves – the self that regrets a past action and the self that took the action in the first place." –Marshall Rosenberg**

MEPSS Activities

Mental – Mindfulness* is available to you every moment of every day. Choose an object as a symbol to remind you to pause, tune into the moment, breathe, and observe what is there for you. Start with 1 minute, then work up slowly until you can stay in a state of mindfulness for 5 minutes. (or more!)

Emotional – To improve your understanding of yourself, take a break! Bring to mind a situation in your life that is causing upset, stress or pain. Get in touch with the feelings you are sensing and say the following phrases from Kristen Neff* to yourself (it is helpful to memorize these for the next time), 'This is a moment of suffering (or upset, stress or hurt).' This will activate mindfulness. Then say, 'Suffering is a part of life.' You may want to put your hands across your heart or offer some self-soothing touch. You can also say, 'I am not alone' or 'We all struggle.' Third, say, 'May I be kind to myself.' Notice the relief and gentle shift you sense to a calmer, more self-compassionate you.

Physical – Choose a place in your body that you feel insecure or embarrassed about, don't like, or don't think is 'good enough.' Notice how you feel and the emotions that arise when you think about that place. Let yourself experience the feelings and let them flow without any thought or story attached to them. Now, offer compassion to that part, accept it, act kindly toward it, offer it love, and be grateful for that part that has contributed to your growth and acceptance of who you are today. Then offer a gesture of love and Self-Compassion to that part. If you wish, you can choose more than one part. The more you can do, the easier Self-Compassion will become.

Social – The best way to provide Self-Compassion is by treating yourself like you would a good friend. Ask yourself, 'What would I say to my friend if they were in the position I am experiencing?' Take note of a few things, then get a mirror and put it where the friend would be sitting across from you and say those things to yourself in the same loving, caring, and nurturing way you would to your friend.

Spiritual – One way to dispel false beliefs and eliminate critical self-talk is to connect to your Divine Self*. It is the source of all light and life within you and your true motivation for living. Spend time in silence in a quiet place listening for that Divine* voice, sensing the divine light energy that is present as you commune together.

Self-Compassion

Self-Confidence

Self-Confidence is the gift of a giant gemstone necklace you wear that glistens and shines as you act from knowing your inherent worth and value.

Self-Confidence is the courage to know yourself, believe in yourself, and commit to acting courageously on your beliefs. Self-Confidence shows that you value yourself for who you are regardless of your imperfections and mistakes. You know that you are worthy of other people's respect and friendship.

Having Self-Confidence does not mean that you believe yourself to be perfect or think you should be. It does not mean that you are Selfish in the wounding sort of possessive way, but that you are selfish in how you treat yourself in a nurturing, caring manner. You do not hold yourself to unrealistic expectations and standards and you certainly don't live a life free of difficulties, problems, or pain. In fact, Self-Confidence is what helps you cope with all these. You are free from Self-Doubt.

Self-Confidence is similar to other Self-Wonderfuls such as Self-Acceptance, Self-Esteem, Self-Efficacy, Self-Love, Self-Regard, and Self-Trust. Self-Confidence emphasizes accepting your whole self and how you act in the world; it's about the quality of life you create for yourself. You have a feeling of being complete, experience a sense of inner peace, have the ability to create and experience happiness, and operate from a balance between your strengths and weaknesses. Put simply, you believe in yourself.

A lack of Self-Confidence creates a negative impact on your life. You feel apathetic, inferior, and unworthy and experience anxiety, depression, and other mental health challenges. You may experience other Self-Woundings, such as Self-Doubt, Self-Humiliation, and Self-Sabotage.

When you are confident in your abilities and feel good about your capabilities, you are more committed, energized, and motivated to take action and achieve your goals. You experience greater enjoyment in life and your activities. When you are relaxed and confident, you have a more enjoyable time interacting with others at social gatherings, and others feel at ease around you.

You gain Self-Confidence when you leave your comfort zone and commit to experiencing new challenges. When you make mistakes and fail, you learn that the fear itself will summon an unknown courage to take over. Courage gives you the strength to depend on yourself and make it through. This can feel invigorating and empowering and contributes to even greater Self-Confidence. To build Self-Confidence, wear that giant gemstone necklace that glitters and shines as you act from knowing your inherent worth and value.

When I breathe, I inhale Self-Confidence and exhale fear and timidity.

I am a Self-Confident, creative, and capable person.

I face difficult situations with Self-Confidence, courage, and conviction and find a way out.

"Self-confidence is the best outfit. Rock it and Own it."
–Anonymous

"The self-confidence one builds from achieving difficult things and accomplishing goals is the most beautiful thing of all."
–Madonna

"Self-confidence is the most attractive quality a person can have. How can anyone see how great you are if you can't see it yourself?" –Kushandwizdom

MEPSS Activities

Mental – Practice mindfulness* by bringing awareness to yourself and your surroundings. Notice your breath flowing in and out and the many sensations of your body. Then let your eyes notice what is in your visual field. Let your ears hear what they are hearing. Let your nose smell what is around you. Let your tongue touch the roof of your mouth and conjure up a flavor you love to taste. Touch a part of your body. Go beyond these sensations to feel the energy, the quiet, and the noises surrounding you. Feel your presence in the here and now and silently, with your inner voice, express confidence in yourself, and give yourself an inner smile and outward hug.

Emotional – Imagine riding a roller coaster of ups and downs between Self-Confidence and Self-Doubt. As you approach the high points, notice the emotions and feelings that come from feeling Self-Confidence. As you descend into the low points, notice the emotions and feelings that arise. Then pivot toward the higher point again and notice what you did to make it happen. Use this at any time to take you to a healthier emotional place.

Physical – A great way to feel Self-Confidence is through confident body postures or 'power poses.' Practice standing tall like royalty waving from a palace balcony, feel your feet firmly on the ground, and keep your body relaxed and open (which might be the hard part, as when we try to stand tall, we strain and tighten). Experiment, have fun, and play with different poses and gestures, both bodily and non-verbal ones. Smile, wave, frown, make a funny face, etc. Try standing on a makeshift podium, dais, stage, or top of a staircase, and sense the shifts in your Self-Confidence. Then choose one or two and hold them for 1-2 minutes (perhaps even take a selfie) to develop body memory to recall at any time you need a boost in Self-Confidence.

Social – A sense of belonging within our social system is fundamental to your well-being. Yet you might struggle to ask for help for fear of rejection or being seen as incompetent. When you ask for help, you can see your efforts flourish in ways you could never achieve on your own. Doing an act of kindness produces the single-most reliable increase in momentary well-being than anything else! Think of one small, simple gesture of kindness you can offer someone or a group, then do it!

Spiritual – Find a place that has stained glass windows. Look at them from outside and then from inside with the sun coming through. Stand in the sun's warmth and notice the effect the colors, design, light, and warmth have on you. Imagine this divine light is also within you, boosting your confidence and allowing you to shine in all your magnificence. If you can, find a keepsake made of glass or crystal that you can use to replicate or remind you of the power of confidence and light.

Self-
Confidence

Self-Conscious

Self-Conscious is the gift of your I AM, the healthy awareness of your own intimate essence and 'beingness'. When it becomes 'intense', it becomes a Self-Wounding.

Being Self-Conscious as a Self-Wonderful means that you are aware of yourself as an individual 'being', in and of yourself, with all parts of your personality, feelings, qualities, and desires connected. Addressing all aspects of yourself is essential. Seeing the connection between all of them helps the tendency to separate out an aspect to focus on which leads to a distorted self-consciousness. The more you can embrace all parts of yourself as a sign of strength, the stronger you will feel in everything you do.

Being Self-Conscious is required to fit in as a social being in a social world.

When you are Self-Conscious in a healthy way, you honor your personal beliefs and values, perform better at work or school, take pride in your accomplishments, take on new challenges, can focus outward easily, maintain healthy relationships, enjoy interacting in social environments, follow the rules, take responsibility, apologize for mistakes, and experience your emotions in healthy moderation.

As a Self-Wounding, being Self-Conscious is seen as an 'intense' or excessive awareness of yourself, as you constantly think about how you act and appear to others and what they think of you. It feels like your every moment is being scrutinized by yourself and an 'audience' of your own making. Your thoughts run wild. Your emotions are bombarded by biochemicals that cause further emotional reactions and responses. This results in agitation, anger, anxiety, awkwardness, depression, embarrassment, humiliation, jealousy, nervousness, obsession, shame, shyness, stress, and further self-consciousness. You get stuck focusing inwardly on yourself, feel inferior, and everything begins to revolve around you as you try to monitor your thoughts and behavior with little success. This can lead to serious mental health issues that are best dealt with by seeking professional help.

Everyone feels Self-Conscious and experiences uncomfortable Self-Conscious moments. You are not alone. Learning to be Self-Conscious in a healthy way is a vital part of everyday life. It allows you to be aware of yourself and your surroundings. It calls you to pay attention to and honor your strengths. It allows you to think before you act rather than acting on instinct. It helps you consider the consequences of your actions and control your emotions so that you can behave in a socially acceptable way. To become more Self-Conscious in healthy, supportive ways, you can also use other Self-Wonderfuls to support your growth and learning and practice the gift of your unique essence, and 'beingness' I AM.

I choose to feel good about myself today and always.

I let my strengths shine and support me.

I embrace and honor all parts of myself.

"It is only when you have become that true Self, consciously, when all these illusions have fallen away, that you will be perfectly free and perfectly happy." –Frederick Lenz

"If you know that someone is going to hear what you're doing, you're always going to be self-conscious about it. In a way that's good; it spurs you on." –Doug Martsch

"When we are self-conscious, we cannot be wholly aware; we must throw ourselves out first. This throwing ourselves away is the act of creativity." –Madeleine L 'Engle

MEPSS Activities

Mental – In a cartoon 'chain thought bubble,'* draw 5 illogical, ridiculous things your thoughts tell you. Stop agreeing with your unhealthy and unsupportive thoughts. Take back control by sticking to the facts. Say back to the thoughts in the chain, 'This is not true. You are just a thought.' Then, with a realistic, compassionate point of view, thank the thought for their viewpoint and come up with 3 scenarios that would turn the situation into a gift and opportunity. Be creative and have fun with this. It will show you the ridiculousness of the original thoughts and lead to dismissing them earlier next time.

Emotional –To act from a healthy place of being Self-Conscious, you must accept and act from your authentic, Simply Self-Wonderful self by being honest, choosing to be true to yourself, and letting your true self be seen. See Brene Brown's* definition of vulnerability* as a sign of strength. The more you can practice 'showing up and being seen' and being honest with your feelings, the more you can grow as a healthy Self-Conscious person. Picture a situation that could benefit from your being vulnerable in this way. Draw a simple picture of yourself standing in your vulnerability and adding a list of strengths underneath like a foundation so you can feel what standing in your power of vulnerability is like and can call on it next time you need it. Working with a therapist* to discover healthy coping strategies is often a good option if you feel challenged, overwhelmed, and 'controlled' by unhealthy emotions.

Physical – 'Throw yourself away' by listing 25 ways you can be creative, enjoy the moment, laugh, and respond to unhealthy Self-Conscious moments. Remember, you can't control how others view you, so get over it!

Social – Believe it or not, other people are not thinking about you as much as you think they are! List 10 Self-Conscious fears that take away your power. Then play the 'So what?' game by treating yourself as you would one of your friends. Imagine hearing your friend's voice asking, 'So what?' or 'What difference does it make? (None!) to 3 of the Self-Conscious fears on your list. Picture your friend's facial expressions and bodily gestures as each is countered. Then repeat these each time you have a Self-Conscious fear that takes away your power. You might also want to create a loving gesture to offer yourself to reinforce this new response.

Spiritual – Take the focus off yourself by seeing yourself with true humility, the ability to know yourself as the Divine Benevolent Source of Love* created you and knows you to be without the exaggerated approval or disapproval you or others place on your sense of worth or acceptance. From this perspective of expansive awareness, offer a prayer or gesture of gratitude for each of the 25 characteristics of the uniquely you that are the gift of your I AM.

self conscious
I AM

Self-Determination

Self-Determination is the gift of being the puppeteer that motivates and manages the strings of your own life.

Self-Determination is the power to control your own destiny by thinking for yourself, without outside influence. It's using your own attitudes and abilities to make confident decisions, set goals, manage, and motivate yourself to take the actions needed to reach your goals and be in charge of your own life. Self-Determination can also refer to a group of people's right to choose their political destiny.

Self-Determination is important because it is connected to needs for autonomy, competence, and relatedness. When these are fulfilled, you are happier and can feel more responsible for your life and the outcomes you want to achieve. You are always seeking to grow, gain mastery over challenges, and develop your sense of self. At the same time, you have a need for autonomy and independence. The interplay between the need for growth as a human being and the need for autonomy and independence is where the learning lies. This plays into your overall health, and especially your psychological health.

Self-Determination focuses primarily on internal sources of motivation, such as gaining independence and wanting to prove yourself, rather on outside factors such as acclaim, fame, money, and other visible signs. Self-Determination is done for self-satisfaction, and enjoyment, rather than an outer reward.

Self-Determination is driven by meeting three basic needs. The first is *competence*; having sufficient intellect, judgement, skill, and strength to perform a given task or feel a sense of mastery as goals are achieved and success is attained. The second is *relatedness*, which is feeling a sense of belonging and closeness to other people, as well as feeling respected and cared for without being undermined by cliques, competition, or criticism by others. The third need is *autonomy*; the ability to govern yourself and be independent. You have choice, and do not feel threatened by others when they try to take away or undermine your power.

Self-Determination is important in education, sports, and the workplace as you feel supported to explore, take the initiative, implement solutions, and reach the goals you've set. You need many skills to excel, many of which are related to making choices, decisions, and problem solving. Other skills have more to do with self-regulation. When you believe you have control over your own life and are inwardly motivated to act and find social support, then you are the puppeteer that motivates and manages the strings of your own life.

I am free to choose my life's direction.

I am motivated and empowered to live my best life.

I am confident in my ability to succeed.

"The new definition of freedom today is self-determination." –John Hope Bryant

"You combine hard work, creativity, and self-determination, and things start to happen." –Sophia Amoroso

"My idea of feminism is self-determination, and it's very open-ended: every woman has the right to become herself and do whatever she needs to do." –Ani DiFranco

MEPSS Activities

Mental – Rank 10 of the most important things in your life. Ask yourself, 'Why is it in this order? What makes #1 more important than #2? Continue to #10. 'What does this tell me about myself?' Then ask yourself, 'Do I want to change the order or work on making one or two more important?' Keep asking questions that lead to more questions. Note the discoveries about yourself and the growth occurring in your life as you focus on your Self-Determination.

Emotional – Create a Self-Determination Council, those subpersonalities of you that motivate, problem-solve, celebrate, and cheer you on, as well as those that act as Saboteurs*. You can start with 4 to 7, then add to them as you discover more. Give them fun names identifying their role in your emotional and decision-making life. Draw pictures or caricatures of them. Take time to be with this aspect of yourself, list the qualities of each, the gifts they offer, and listen to the wants and most essential need*. When you get to an emotionally stuck place or feel overwhelmed, ask yourself, 'Who in me is feeling so (name the emotion or feeling) right now? Then imagine giving that subpart what it needs from your highest place of Self-Determination. Thank it for being part of you, your growth, and your Self-Determination.

Physical – Map out your imagined future on a life timeline*gameboard. Imagine your future life with circles for each step along the way to the finish line of success. What does the finish line of success look like for you? What are the goals you need to achieve to get there? Map it out year by year for as many years as you wish. What first action step can you take today to start the momentum and motivate you toward reaching your first goal? When you complete your first action step, offer yourself a small reward, then continue to take the next step and the next, celebrating in small ways each successful step. And if you take a step or two or a few backward, the reward comes in the learning and will still help you as you gain Self-Determination.

Social – You are the 'Self' in Self-Determination. You make the changes needed for your highest growth and transformation. Yet you are not alone and are influenced by other people and social systems. Who are your top 5 influencers? What qualities and characteristics have you brought into your life for support from each of them? Then ask, 'Who did I expect to change instead of doing the work myself? How did that keep me from doing my Self-Determination work?' Journal your answers and thoughts. If you want to talk it through with someone, do so for more Self-Discovery and support.

Spiritual – Remember, 'All things are possible for those who believe.' Believe in yourself. Have faith* in yourself, your vision, dedication, hard work, Self-Determination, and your ability to achieve your goals. Faith* works subconsciously, helping you move toward your goal. If you lack faith and believe the opposite, you'll defeat yourself. Act as if you already have what you want by telling yourself the story of your dreams coming true. Make a picture book with each page showing a step of success and on the final page showing the attained goal. You can draw it yourself, use computer graphics, or pictures from magazines.

Self Determination
Self Determination
Self Determination
Self Determination

Self-Discipline

Self-Discipline is the gift of your personal, loving guidebook of rules and practices that trains you in the staying power to reach your goals and achieve your dreams.

Self-Discipline is using your willpower to establish a pattern of behavior. It's following through with your tasks, goals, and dreams. It acts in favor of some greater gain, good plan, or results, even if it requires more effort and time. Self-Discipline is not punitive or restrictive, as some conclude, but rather confirms an inner strength and staying power that gives you control over any situation.

Self-Discipline can appear as the ability to make decisions and plans despite inconvenience, hardship, or obstacles. It helps you overcome the indecisiveness, laziness, and procrastination that can easily deter you. It requires thinking before acting, enduring, finishing what you started, showing restraint, and avoiding unhealthy excesses that could lead to damaging consequences for yourself, another, or the planet.

Self-Discipline is developed over a lifetime. As the name suggests, it is not easy. It often causes some discomfort and resistance and may be difficult, unpleasant, and require a great deal of effort or even sacrifice. It takes constant focus and work to progress and succeed because you have to override your more basic desires and go against outside influences and pressure to take the easy way out of an opportunity, situation, or life in general.

Despite the hard work and discipline it involves, exercising and attaining Self-Discipline can be fun, easy, can become a habit, and can bring benefits beyond what you originally imagined. Self-Discipline is similar to another Self-Wonderful, Self-Control, which includes having the personal initiative to start and the stamina to persevere. Self-Discipline uses your personal, loving guidebook of rules and practices and trains you in the staying power to reach your goals and achieve your dreams.

I have the self-discipline to accomplish my goals and reach my dreams.

I have the self-discipline to work through any challenge the day might bring.

I am in control and can ignore distractions and achieve today's tasks.

"Self-discipline is the magic power that makes you virtually unstoppable." –Anonymous

"I think self-discipline is something; it's like a muscle. The more you exercise it, the stronger it gets." –Daniel Goldstein

"Self-Discipline begins with mastery of your thoughts. If you don't control what you think, you can't control what you do." –Napoleon Hill

MEPSS Activities

Mental – Be aware of your thoughts just before caving into a craving, desire, harmful habit, or temptation. Make a list of 5 situations you wrestle with. Then list 10 justifications your mind uses to weaken your willpower and Self-Discipline. Now, write a new thought that encourages Self-Discipline and the benefits you truly desire.

Emotional – What is one thing you often don't feel like doing but is necessary for your health and life? What do those feelings tell you? What is the resistance underneath the feelings? Now instead of a 'should do,' what can you say to yourself that shifts the feelings to something preferable or beneficial to do? What are three benefits? Remind yourself of these when the situation arises the next time.

Physical – In an area of your choice, establish a strategy and action plan to make it difficult to access a particular temptation and increase Self-Discipline. What is your goal? What are the long-term rewards? What is the first step you will take? What is the second step? What is the third? After you've taken these steps, will you have the motivation to continue one step at a time? When you have reached your goal, celebrate in an affirming and healthy way.

Social – Planet earth is in peril because of the overconsumption and lack of Self-Discipline we individually and collectively have practiced over the years. What area is most concerning to you? Find an organization or group that is doing something in that area and volunteer to be an advocate and perhaps even an activist. Join others in raising sustainable practices to heal and restore our precious and wonderful earth.

Spiritual – Often, in hard or tempting situations, you must reach outside yourself to find the willpower or energy to commit to Self-Discipline. Many faith traditions encourage faith* and trust in a Divine/God/Higher Power/Mystery/Source/Universe* that is always available to you. What source, power, or energy do you rely on? How do you call on it for use? What does it offer you? If you don't have one, ask a friend about theirs or explore faith and spiritual traditions that interest or call out to you.

Self-Discipline
Self-Discipline
Self-Discipline
Self-Discipline
Self-Discipline
Self-Discipline
Self-Discipline
Self-Discipline

Self-Discovery

Self-Discovery is the gift of an adventurous treasure hunt you lead using all the clues that you are to actualize your unique potential and live the life you want to live.

Self-Discovery is a journey inward to understand and embrace your authentic self. In essence, this is what personal growth is all about. It views life as your teacher and uses any life experience as an opportunity to grow, expand your perspective, move past any limits, and find the paths you want to pursue in your outer life. This inward journey is a time of self-examination and reflection of your thoughts, beliefs, words, and actions, as well as your abilities, interests, and passions, to reach your own conclusion about who you really are.

Self-Discovery gives your life meaning. Everything in life is here to teach you something and invite you to learn and grow as a person. Self-Discovery helps you become confident in who you are in your uniqueness as a fascinating human being. It helps you create your own reality as you connect to your true self. It helps you heal as you address the issues that have held you back from becoming your full potential. You realize that you aren't a victim of your circumstances but can live an empowered life when you are able to shift your thoughts, beliefs, behaviors, and overall energy to align with what you want to become. And it helps you to never feel alone. When you are purposely learning about yourself, you connect with who you truly are, feel comfortable with yourself, and naturally start to enjoy your own company and truly love yourself at all times.

Don't be afraid to admit who you are and accept your limitations. Whatever lies hidden inside you will benefit from the light of Self-Discovery. When darker things show up, things like fear, doubts, or what you may label as negative, this exposure will help you acknowledge them, begin to shine light on them, accept them with love, practice patience with yourself, deal with them, and transform them into something that makes you stronger as they become gifts. When you find more helpful things, like strengths, skills, abilities, and talents, that already seem like gifts, don't be afraid to use them to reach your highest goals.

Your journey to Self-Discovery does not have to be a solo journey. No one lives their life all by themselves. Learning what others are doing on their journey to Self-Discovery can give you ideas, show you new places to explore, and bring support figures and friends to help each other along the way. So, make sure that you connect with others and discover yourself as one part of the interconnected world.

Only through the discovery of self can you identify your purpose and actualize your potential. Your adventure is to accept whatever you discover and continue the treasure hunt to move forward in your quest for Self-Discovery.

I am transforming into someone who is always developing, discovering, and learning.

I am always developing myself in every area of my life.

I discover something new about myself each day.

"There is no greater journey than the one that you must take to discover all of the mysteries that lie within you."
–Michelle Sandlin

"The delights of self-discovery are always available."
–Gail Sheehy

"After all these years, I am still involved in the process of self-discovery. It's better to explore life and make mistakes than to play it safe. Mistakes are part of the dues one pays for a full life." –Sophia Loren

MEPSS Activities

Mental – Being yourself is important, but knowing yourself is even more important and necessary to understand who you are and what you want to get out of life. Expand your mind. Choose a book about the discovery of self that offers new concepts and ideas, expands your curiosity, and cultivates an open mind.

Emotional – Reflect on who you are or who you want to become. Write what emerges in a journal and create a symbol that you can use to keep you moving toward that vision.

Physical – As you begin to know yourself more deeply, your lifestyle changes, and you begin to feel better about yourself. Your physical body wants to express this new you. And you also want to become physically healthier. Choose one food-oriented or physical activity to start giving your body what it truly needs.

Social – Learn what other people do on their quest for Self-Discovery by volunteering at a social service organization or charity for one day or shift. Talk with others as you are together, and be grateful for what each person, including you, has to offer.

Spiritual – Explore your spiritual side by choosing a religious tradition to learn more about. Visiting a place of worship – a church, synagogue, mosque, meeting place, or nature. Pray or meditate about your place in the universe and see what questions and answers come. Compare your journey of the body to the journey of the soul.

SELF DISCOVERY

Self-Efficacy

Self-Efficacy is the gift of rising up with all your moxie to conquer anything life throws your way.

Self-Efficacy is believing in yourself. It's having control over your own functioning and the events that affect your life. Self-Efficacy believes in your own ability to succeed, and it plays a role in how you think, act, and feel about your place in the world. Paying attention to your own mental state and emotional well-being is vital for Self-Efficacy. The more you practice Self-Efficacy and believe in yourself, the more you can develop a deeper interest in the activities that shape your life.

A strong sense of Self-Efficacy creates a stronger commitment to continue pursuing your interests and activities. Self-Efficacy views problems as challenges to be mastered and learned from. Self-Efficacy allows you to recover quickly from setbacks and disappointments, knowing you've got this, even if not on the first try!

When your Self-Efficacy is weak, fear and anxiety undermine your feelings, and you doubt yourself and your abilities. You avoid challenges, believing they are too difficult to overcome, and then quickly lose confidence in your ability to reach your goals. You don't want that, and the world doesn't either!

Fortunately, Self-Efficacy helps determine what goals you choose and how you go about making them happen. Self-Efficacy allows you to remain confident and optimistic even when things become difficult. You can build Self-Efficacy through support and encouragement and by watching other people succeed through hard work. Watching others can also motivate you to try something you haven't felt fully comfortable trying and builds resilience as you believe more and more in yourself and increase your Self-Efficacy. Self-Efficacy is supported by other Self-Wonderfuls such as Self-Confidence and Self-Esteem. Self-Efficacy says you have the power and control to create and seek opportunities to help you master difficult skills, complete challenging tasks, find positive role models, and listen to encouraging and motivating people. As you do this and take care of your mental health, you can assert that gift of moxie that is you, rising up to conquer any challenges life brings your way!

I use my Jedi-like power to rise up and conquer this challenge with easy-peasy, I've-got-this-confidence, and determination!

I act and succeed at any endeavor I set my mind to.

I have the power inside me to conquer anything life brings my way.

"To really boost your sense of self-efficacy, think of ways you could modify your usual tasks to suit your personal style." –Martha Beck

"If self-efficacy is lacking, people tend to behave ineffectually, even though they know what to do." –Albert Bandura

"Incongruities between self-efficacy and action stem from misperceptions of task demands as much as from faulty self-knowledge." –Albert Bandura

MEPSS Activities

Mental – Pay attention to your thoughts. If you are getting stressed or nervous, say the above affirmation to calm down and center yourself. It will give you the courage to go for it because you know you are really and truly great!

Emotional – When emotions such as fear and anxiety show up, rather than trying to push them away, welcome them as friends and allies with the power you can tap into and use. Visualize yourself succeeding with each step, like an inchworm slowly making its way across a path. Use the Fingerhold for Emotions video.*

Physical – Choose a simple, new task you've always wanted to try. Take the first step, then the next, and so on until you complete it. Take as much time as you need. Celebrate each step of your success with something small but wonderful that you can easily give yourself, like a hug, a 5 minute 'playtime' reward, or another simple gift to congratulate yourself.

Social – Sign up for a class, webinar, or course that you've always dreamed of taking. Join with others and let them cheer you on as you cheer them on as you all succeed!

Spiritual – List the qualities and experiences that have helped you succeed in the past. Offer appreciation for your Self-Efficacy wonderfulness and gratitude for the countless others (you can name a few) that have contributed to your learning, Self-Efficacy, and success.

Self-
Efficacy

Self-Empowerment

Self-Empowerment is the gift of being the driver of your own life and steering it to the life you want most.

Self-Empowerment is simply becoming powerful, taking control of your own life, and making positive choices to achieve your goals and success. It means you know who you are, understand your strengths, and know where you can improve. It means you believe in yourself and your power, and how you are likely to respond to situations. Your skills and abilities are the main resources that enable you to achieve your goals. They can be learned through education, experience, practice, and training. When acting from Self-Empowerment, you change the impact you have on yourself, others, the events in your life, and the world around you.

When you lack Self-Empowerment, you tend to lack control over what you do and allow others to make decisions for you. You feel frustrated and feel stuck, unable to communicate what you want and need, and instead give in to what others think is 'best' for you. Disempowerment creates a sense of obligation and an imbalanced relationship that creates stress and strain. You must learn to take back and own your power, whatever that looks like for you.

Self-Empowerment doesn't mean you have to go it alone or feel that things should come to you automatically. Rather Self-Empowerment means that you are willing to work hard, try new things, reflect, and assess what needs to be done, then do it. It usually requires making some fundamental changes in your beliefs, behaviors, values, and actions, which is not an easy process, especially if you have relied on others for a long time. At first, you may not see much of a difference, but even small changes will take hold and result in greater confidence, power, and success in the future.

Self-Empowerment will help you see the brighter side of life. It will improve your overall health because you will see yourself in a much clearer way, with less need for worrisome emotions and comparisons. It allows you to have healthier relationships because you won't need others to tell you how capable and amazing you are. It will enhance your work in the world as you will be able to make decisions easily because you know your desires, purpose, and values. Along with other Self-Wonderfuls, Self-Empowerment will allow you to be the driver of your own life, do anything you want, and steer you to the life you want most.

I have all the power and strength I need to make my dreams my reality.

I am my best advocate and know what I want in life.

I will triumph over challenges.

"Selecting a challenge and meeting it creates a sense of self-empowerment that becomes the ground for further successful challenges." –Julia Cameron

"Taking initiative is a form of self-empowerment." –Stephen Covey

"You are living in a time when opportunities for self-empowerment, expanded awareness, and spiritual growth appear to be unlimited." –Barbara Marciniak

MEPSS Activities

Mental – Talk with someone you trust or spend time journaling or another way you reflect on things, asking yourself: 'What painful situation or memory has caused a disempowering belief to form that has gotten in the way of new growth, freedom, and Self-Empowerment? How is it harming me? What new Self-Empowering belief can I replace it with?' Write the new Self-Empowering belief in places where you can refer to it often.

Emotional – Try something new that you have wanted to do but haven't given yourself a chance to do. It may be an educational course, hobby, task, or daring outdoor sports activity that previously you haven't felt you could do. Remind yourself that it's the process, not necessarily the outcome, that teaches you the most.

Physical – Exercise can be fun! It doesn't have to be arduous or strenuous; you just have to do it regularly! What form of exercise will you choose to make your body strong and your mind clear? What date will you begin? What motivating factors will you need to start? What equipment will you need? Have fun with this and invite a friend to join you!

Social – Make a list of 5 people you admire who are Self-Empowered. Who are they? What do they do to show their Self-Empowerment? How did they grow their strength and skills? Choose one to look into deeper, and if you feel inspired, write them, and let them know you are an admirer!

Spiritual – Make a collage of things you know about yourself, things you love, hate, your dreams, passions, what makes you laugh, and what makes you cry. Look at your collage often, especially when you feel you are becoming disempowered, and let it empower you again.

SELF EMPOWERMENT

Self-Esteem

Self-Esteem is the gift of attitude that acts as a magnifying glass, enlarging as you appreciate and value who you are, and shrinking as a Self-Wounding when you think less of yourself.

Self-Esteem is related to many of the other Self-Wonderfuls and has a direct relationship with your overall well-being. Believing in yourself and accepting yourself for who you are provides you with the motivation to find fulfillment in life. It can involve a variety of beliefs you have about yourself, your appearance, your capabilities, behaviors, and anything that contributes to making you feel good, confident, and trusting in yourself. A realistic yet positive view of yourself is considered the ideal.

Self-Esteem influences your life in many ways and is crucial to your happiness, relationships, success, and ability to flourish in life. It changes throughout a lifetime. Successes and setbacks, both personal and professional, can create fluctuations in your feeling of Self-Esteem from minute to minute, even year to year. It varies depending on what you are telling yourself at the moment. For example, the confident person appears to have a strong sense of Self-Esteem and is unafraid to show their curiosity and discuss their experiences, ideas, and opportunities. They can laugh at themselves, see the humor in trying situations, and are comfortable in social settings.

Whereas a steady diet of disapproval from family, friends, teachers, coworkers, and supervisors, as well as your own thoughts influenced by others, can erode your fragile Self-Esteem, causing feelings of value and worthiness to plummet, leading to feeling defeated, depressed, or other signs of low Self-Esteem. Self-Esteem may let you down whenever you fail or feel inadequate because you have not claimed and owned all parts of you and accepted you for who you are.

When you feel let down, you can use another Self Wonderful, Self-Compassion, to help you care for yourself. That's the difference between the two. Self-Esteem is about thinking you are worthy, and thoughts about yourself can change at any time based on what you are experiencing. Self-Compassion steps in precisely when Self-Esteem lets you down, and you cannot claim the thoughts that can move you back toward fully accepting yourself.

It's normal to go through times when you feel down about yourself and good about yourself. So, in general, Self-Esteem stays in a range that reflects how you feel about yourself overall.

The strongest single factor in prosperity consciousness is Self-Esteem: believing you can do it, believing you deserve it, believing you will get it. So, instead of shrinking when you think less of yourself, use Self-Esteem as a magnifying glass, enlarging as you appreciate and value who you are.

I am competent, smart, and able to find success and fulfillment in my life.

I love the person I am becoming, and I celebrate myself!

I let go of my harmful feelings and accept all that is good.

"Self-esteem isn't everything; it's just that there's nothing without it." –Gloria Steinem

"My self-esteem is high because I honor who I am." –Louise Hay

"There are people with modest jobs, unspectacular bodies, and unglamorous friends, who confidently nevertheless lay claim to buoyant levels of self-esteem." –The School of Life, Self-Esteem, YouTube

MEPSS Activities

Mental –What do you believe about yourself that just isn't true? Or is partly true? What are others who have no way of knowing the truth you're saying about yourself isn't true? Make a 'mind-map'* of a thought by connecting other thoughts that come from that thought to see the pattern you are creating. See if there is one thought that you can begin to shift or remove entirely and notice what happens to all the other connecting thoughts. Do they stay the same? Do they disappear? Do they shift into something else? You have the choice to make them into whatever you want!

Emotional –One of the biggest things that gets in the way of healthy Self-Esteem is feeling the need to be a perfectionist, which is impossible. We all make mistakes, many of them, throughout each day. Think of a time when you made a mistake. How did this help you grow, learn, and strengthen your Self-Esteem?

Physical – To develop an honest and realistic picture of yourself, take a Self-Esteem inventory by writing down 10 of your strengths and 10 of your weaknesses. Ask one of the strengths: How can you assist me in lifting up one of my weaknesses? You can do more if you like. You may find that the strengths and weaknesses overlap, and you may notice there is more help in your strengths than you ever imagined for your so-called weaknesses!

Social – Comparing yourself to others is a trap that is easy to fall into. So, stop comparing yourself to others and compare yourself to you! Use photos of yourself and look back 1 month, 6 months, 1 year, 2 years, 5 years, and recall where you were then with your Self-Esteem and where you are now. Take a picture of yourself and add it to the collection as a chronicle of your growth and maturity.

Spiritual – Make a collage or other creative piece that expresses you with your highest Self-Esteem for all to see. Put it somewhere you can see it every day. Celebrate YOU!

Self-Esteem

Self-Expression

Self-Expression is the gift of connecting your personal, public relations person with the world to show yourself in creative and fulfilling ways.

Self-Expression might be one of the most important ways to connect to others, display your individuality, show your true character, shine your spirit, and allow others to see the totality of who you are. It forms the basis of your personality. It sets the tone for your entire life and is vital to pay attention to, especially if you want to feel more understood and valued for who you are.

When who you are and your view of the world is acknowledged, heard, and seen, then you can see that you are not alone with your inner thoughts. Self-Expression transfers the energy from your feelings and thoughts into another form. This gives you the courage to be the best you can be and express your authentic self in a wide variety of forms: actions, body movements and dance, clothing and accessories, decorating and design, facial expressions, music, photography, possessions, speaking, writing, words, the work you do, and an unlimited variety of creative expressions that are uniquely you.

Self-Expression encourages you to work more effectively and collaboratively with others. It excites, inspires, and motivates you to keep sharing yourself and all you have to offer in a particular situation and in general. It makes you feel good and can be extremely therapeutic, offers a healthy form of escape for a while, helps you manage your emotions, observe a situation from a distance, shift your mood, and soothe your conscious and unconscious mind. Self-Expression is a wonderful tool in your emotional healing process.

Self-Expression is about being transparent about who you are, not in a bragging sort of way or in an intentionally hurtful way, but in a kind way that tells people the truth about who you are and how you feel, without leaving out anything important unsaid in your relationships. In some cultures, this may be considered unusual, looked down upon, seen as selfish, or even a waste of time. Yet most agree that Self-Expression is vital for happiness, Self-Fulfillment, and peace. Self-Expression can be seen as the ultimate form of generosity as you share all you are with the world in creative and fulfilling ways as your own public relations person.

I am filled with infinite possibilities for Self-Expression.

I open my life to the energy of creative Self-Expression.

I am wonderfully expressive and creative.

"Neuroscience is teaching us that self-expression might be one – if not the most important ways for people to connect, navigate, and grow with each other." –Judith Glaser

"Perfect self-expression will never be labor, but of such absorbing interest that it will almost seem like play." –Florence Scovel Shinn

"If we're really committed to growth, we never stop discovering new dimensions of self and self-expression." – Oprah Winfrey

MEPSS Activities

Mental – Decorate the outside of a paper bag or cardboard box with images and words representing the qualities you show to the outside world. Decorate the inside of the paper bag or box with images or words representing the inner qualities you keep hidden from most people. Then ask yourself, 'Which qualities from the inside of the paper bag or cardboard box am I now willing to share with the outside world?' Figure out a way to share it and share it in your own unique way, of course!

Emotional – Share details about something in your day with another person and how it made you feel. If you don't have another person to share it with, write a poem and post it on social media.

Physical – Go wild, have fun, make yourself smile, and express yourself in the unique clothes you wear! Make sure you take a selfie and post it on social media or put it somewhere you can see and smile at it often!

Social – Find a public space and initiate a group creative collaboration by placing one item with a note for others to add one thing to. Monitor it over the day or week and see what it becomes. Share what you are doing with friends and the community on social media or even contact the local newspaper or television station to cover it as a human-interest story. Don't forget to take a picture of it along the way.

Spiritual – Spend 1 hour in silence with some modeling clay. Let your fingers and hands create something that expresses you. Don't think about it beforehand, judge it during the process, or evaluate it when you are finished. Just let it be. Later, spend more time in silence with your finished work and listen for what it says about your Self-Expressive self.

Self
Expression

Self-Fulfillment

Self-Fulfillment is the feel-good gift of a happy face as you realize your hopes, ambitions, and full potential.

Self-Fulfillment is a state of being in which you have what you want and need nothing more to feel satisfied. It generally does not come from material things. It comes from you and only you, the only one responsible for your ultimate happiness and fulfillment. It involves your mindset and living a life focused on the few things that increase your quality of life and bring you happiness, no matter what comes your way. It means using your time and attention in ways that matter in the long run to live your chosen best life. Yes, this is challenging, and it is also extremely rewarding! Are you up for the challenge? Are you ready to open the gifts?

To feel a greater sense of Self-Fulfillment, find the good in every moment, even while acknowledging the difficult and disappointing moments. Bring an attitude of curiosity about what the gift might be in the situation. This lets you identify the areas in your life where changes could be made to move you closer to your ambitions, hopes, full potential, and Self-Fulfillment. It allows you to have rich, diverse, unexpected experiences that deeply matter to you. You live each day with a healthy mix of excitement, fun, good stress, and joy, as well as challenges and struggles that keep you growing and Self-Fulfilled. You may shift priorities and goals as you become more and more aligned with your true self. Only you can determine what is fulfilling for you.

Self-Fulfillment is often hindered by trying to achieve someone else's idea of what would be best for you. When you cave into society's expectations or fake happiness for someone else's sake, you become disappointed, live life minimally, and often use material things to try to satisfy a deeper yearning for Self-Fulfillment, thus making it more unclear about who you are and what you need for true Self-Fulfillment.

Self-Fulfillment must be distinguished from a self-fulfilling prophecy. A self-fulfilling prophecy is a belief, expectation, or 'prediction' you hold about a future event that becomes real because you continue to believe or anticipate that it will come true. It suggests that your beliefs influence your actions, and indeed they do. So be careful. A self-fulfilling prophecy can have either beneficial or unhealthy outcomes or consequences.

Self-Fulfillment goes beyond the day-to-day with a sense of completeness that takes a lifetime to achieve. You eagerly intentionally set goals for yourself, visualize, and work toward success even when the going gets tough. You celebrate the small wins and successes on your way to your larger goals and give yourself recognition for your accomplishments. You feel content with life's simpler things and who you are. All of the Self-Wonderfuls will assist you in the feel-good gift of a happy face as you realize your hopes, ambitions, and full potential of Self-Fulfillment.

I have the freedom and power to create a fulfilling life for myself.

Each day I live a more satisfying life and move towards Self-Fulfillment.

I celebrate my accomplishments and realize my full potential.

"We must live a genuine life in order to discover personal happiness and self-fulfillment. Understanding that a person is living a lie is the first step into realizing what is possible. No matter how frightful such a proposition is, we must dare to be an original self." –Kilroy J. Oldster

"People take different roads seeking self-fulfillment and happiness. Just because they're not on your road does not mean they are lost." –Dalai Lama

"What is it we are questing for...There is nothing you can do that's more important than being self-fulfilled. You become a sign, you become a signal, transparent to transcendence; in this way you will find, live, become a realization of your own personal myth." –Joseph Campbell

MEPSS Activities

Mental – What do you believe about life? Make a list of 10 beliefs you hold about how your present life works on this planet. Look at each one and discern if this belief is moving you forward or keeping you stuck. For the ones you're stuck on, how might you shift the belief into one that moves you forward?

Emotional – Recall a time when you had a moment of 'unutterable fulfillment' that could not be expressed in words. What were the feelings, the bodily sensations, the mental awareness, the spiritual revelations, the social implications that prompted you to change forever? Try to immerse yourself in that experience again; just be with it, offering gratitude for the experience and the Self-Fulfillment that occurred. If you haven't had one of these grand 'ah-ha' moments, perhaps there was a smaller one that has continued to shape who you are. Offer gratitude for all your experiences, great and small.

Physical – It is rare to find total Self-Fulfillment in the regular work-a-day world unless you have intentionally chosen to create it for yourself. What are the small things that can give you work satisfaction? What small personal goal can you create to reach fulfillment in some area of your work life that can become significant and powerful when added to other small goals and accomplishments? Take one step toward that goal and celebrate the beginning of Self-Fulfillment!

Social – You have lived much of your life trying to fulfill the expectations of your family, society, and culture. What is one expectation that has led you astray from your true positive purpose because a hidden agenda is attached? What is one shift you can make to create a more empowering motivation to find the true longing of your heart and soul? Find a symbol to express this shift and keep it with you.

Spiritual – Take a walk in nature. Observe nature's beauty and gifts that are there for you. Create a piece of art using seeds, leaves, branches, rocks, sticks, etc., to convey joy, love, fulfillment, hope, or success. You can do it right on the spot and leave it there for others to enjoy, or if it is permissible, take it home and set it up in a place that will catch your heart and eye.

Self Fulfillment
Self Fulfillment
Self Fulfillment
Self Fulfillment

Self-Image

Self-Image is the gift of your inner mirror that is dynamic and changing, expressing how you feel about yourself at any moment.

Self-Image is your personal view of yourself. It is created by your thoughts from early childhood experiences and by how others see you, how you perceive others see you, how you perceive you see yourself, and the way you would like ideal self to be. Self-Image is important because how you think about yourself affects how you interact with others and the world around you. Your Self-Image is not permanent because your thoughts about yourself constantly change. Your Self-Image changes and becomes more stable over your lifetime as you learn to fully accept and love yourself.

A healthy Self-Image can boost your mental, emotional, physical, social, and spiritual well-being as you recognize your assets and potential while being realistic about your limitations and liabilities. A distorted Self-Image can decrease your satisfaction and ability to function in these areas as you focus on your faults and weaknesses by distorting your failures and imperfections.

When you have a healthy Self-Image, you see yourself as attractive, desirable, smart, and intelligent. Looking in the mirror, you see a happy, healthy person reflected there. You have confidence that others see you as you see yourself.

If you have a distorted Self-Image, you have made up a view of yourself that is untrue and not based in reality. You see yourself as unattractive, undesirable, and unintelligent. When you look in the mirror, you see an unhappy, unhealthy person looking back at you. You believe that you are nowhere near your ideal self and that others see you the same way you do. When you feel bad about yourself and your life, it is natural for your perception of yourself to suffer. These feelings often cascade into depression, anxiety, and other emotional or psychological problems. If you become obsessed with your physical appearance, you may develop an eating disorder, want to harm yourself, or feel shame.

You are never a finished 'product.' There is always room to grow, develop, and evolve as you live each day. Consistency is important to keep you steady, so you are not influenced or swayed by other people and their opinions. Be true to yourself! Your growth comes from the gift of your inner mirror that is dynamic and changing, expressing how you feel about yourself at any moment as a beautiful picture expressing the true you in everything you do. So let the world see YOU!

In this moment, I see myself as the best possible me.

I am always growing toward my best self.

The person I see in the mirror is fully loved and accepted in every moment.

"Self-image is the key to human personality and human behavior. Change the self-image and you change the personality and the behavior." –Maxwell Maltz

"A strong, positive self-image is the best possible preparation for success." –Dr. Joyce Brothers

"A positive self-image has little relationship to our material circumstances." –Ezra Taft Benson

MEPSS Activities

Mental – Review your thoughts about yourself as you go about your day. Don't attach a thought or story; just notice them as passing clouds* across the sky of your inner mind. Send love* to them. Notice the ones that affirm and appreciate who you are and the ones that devalue and demean you. Ask for more affirming and appreciative thoughts to replace those devaluing and demeaning you.

Emotional – Look into the mirror and smile, then tell a story about yourself that makes you happy. Then tell one that makes you sad. Then one that makes you joyful. Then one that makes you angry. Then one that that is frivolous and fun. Notice who you are in each story.

Physical – Your body image is a big factor in your self-image. Take a 'self-guided' tour of your body, starting with the top of your head, your hair, your ears, eyes, eyebrows, cheeks, nose, mouth, lips, neck, arms, wrists, hands, fingers, breasts, abdomen, hips, buttocks, legs, ankles, feet, toes, your skin, your overall appearance, and any other aspect of your body that you are drawn to. You can even talk to your organs, glands, tissues, and cells, especially if they have caused you health concerns. Talk to one body part you find difficult to accept. Tell it 3 things that you cannot do without it. Send it love and acceptance for how it makes you the unique person you are!

Social – Get out in the world and do something you have always dreamed of doing. Go a little bit crazy if you want to. Give yourself permission to let the world see you for who you are! Break all the limits you have set for yourself. Go for it! Just do it!

Spiritual – Before bed tonight, list 10 things you like about yourself (or more if that is too easy!) Put the list under your pillow or near your bed. Send an intention that you will wake up in a perfect mood with perfect confidence and willpower to go through your day.

Self-Image

Self-Love

Self-Love is the gift of accepting your value and worth as a perfectly imperfect beloved human being for the purpose of nurturing your own spiritual growth and transformation.

Self-Love is the belief that you are a valuable and worthy person period, without any conditions, for conditional love is no love at all! Self-Love is unconditional, which means rediscovering your true essence, your original self, that amazingly beautiful, caring, gorgeous, magnificent, sensitive, thoughtful, loving, loved, loveable, perfectly imperfect human being that you came into the world as at birth.

Self-Love isn't selfish. Self-Love isn't a luxury; it's necessary to live life fully. Self-Love is much more than a feeling; it's deeper and more eternal than your fluctuating circumstances. Self-Love is something that you must accept, embrace, and learn about intimately, in the unique expression it is for you.

Self-Love is dynamic; it grows through appreciating yourself and taking action that support all areas of your life. Self-Love motivates you to make choices that nurture your well-being and serve you well. It's something that you must practice every moment. Only you can create the life of love you want for yourself.

Allowing yourself to show up as your authentic self is one of the most loving, empowering things you can do. Self-Love makes you a healthier person. When you expand the Self-Love within you and accept yourself as you are, you no longer spend as much time judging yourself and focusing on your weaknesses or the need to explain them away. Instead, you have compassion for yourself as a perfectly imperfect, beloved human being searching for personal meaning, purpose, and value while intentionally living a loving and fulfilling life.

Self-Love makes you a better person, which benefits you and others because loving yourself is also about loving others. You can't love another person until you love yourself. Then, your love for yourself ripples out to others through your beliefs, behaviors, and actions, and influences everything and everyone in its path.

Your greatest life lesson is learning how to fully love yourself. There is no one better to fall in love with than yourself! You are the person who was with you from the very beginning, and you will remain with you until the very end of your unique and wonderful life. The journey takes dedication, devotion, discipline, practice, faith, and trust in yourself. You must remind yourself every day lovingly why you matter. It opens the rich, ever-flowing abundance of light and love all around you. So, practice Self-Love by accepting the gift of your value and worth as a perfectly imperfect beloved human being for the purpose of nurturing your own spiritual growth and transformation!

I love myself always completely and easily.
I love every part of what makes me who I am.
I am a perfectly imperfect beloved child of God.

"Self-love is the source of all other loves." –Pierre Corneille

"Self-love is making sure that every single choice we make in life honors our mind, body, and soul." –Roxana Jones

"Self-love is an ocean and your heart is a vessel. Make it full, and any excess will spill over into the lives of the people you hold dear. But you must come first." –Beau Taplin

MEPSS Activities

Mental – The words you say to yourself profoundly impact all areas of your well-being. Today, notice when the Saboteur voice* tries to come in and diminish and devalue who you are. Make a list of 10 phrases that your Saboteur* tells you regularly. Then replace those phrases with words of affirmation that offer Self-Love. Use them often until they become the dominant response and leave you feeling loved.

Emotional – One of the best ways to begin to practice Self-Love is to spend quality time with yourself. Set aside time each day to be present to Self-Love using deep breathing, meditation, or other self-care activity. Make a deliberate intention to connect to the essence of your true self. Celebrate and show yourself love as you do so.

Physical – Offer Self-Love by taking care of your body. Get a massage, take a hot bath, spend a day at a spa giving yourself the full treatment: facial, manicure, pedicure, whatever sounds luxuriously caring and extraordinarily loving toward yourself!

Social – List 5 things you would like to do to show love to others you love. Then do them for yourself first. If you already do some of them, up the ante and do something even more loving for yourself before serving others. When you've completed those 5 things, make another list of 10 this time and do them! Keep showing Self-Love and, in turn, showing love to others.

Spiritual – Find a picture of yourself as a child before age 5 if possible. Spend a minute or two looking at the picture, noticing the expression in your eyes and face, your hair, how you are holding or moving your arms and hands, and your attitude, posture, and general body movement. Spend time loving you, remembering who you were as your original self, your true essence, you as a perfectly imperfect beloved child. Write 10 adjectives or words that describe who you are here. Then ask the child you are in the picture to offer you as an adult a gift that embodies the essence of who you are. Make a pact to get together often to nurture, support, and show Self-Love to one another.

SELF
LOVE
SELF
LOVE

Self - Portrait

Self-Portrait is the gift of artistry illustrating all of who you are in creative form.

A Self-Portrait is an intimate, bold declaration of identity created by you. You are fascinating; it's who you are. You are infinite, complex, and ever-changing. You are alive, holy, and true! You are a masterpiece and the greatest art you will ever create.

Creating a Self-Portrait inspires you to accept and recognize yourself outside and within. It reveals your beauty, flaws, personality, and intricacies and shows the real you, which isn't easy to capture. It's a statement and proof of your existence and reality and a way to capture yourself at a specific moment in time in your own becoming.

Self Portraits are as old as time and can take many forms. They can be a painting, photograph, sculpture, collage, diary entry, drawing, video, film, cartoon, recorded conversation, creative expression, or computer-generated artwork that expresses the depth of your personality.

Self-Portraits require thought, planning, skill, and effort to create the right mood, edge, light, pose, and scene for everything to come together visually or contextually. They force you to see yourself in a way that is different than just looking in a mirror or snapping a selfie on your phone. In contrast, a selfie is a spontaneous creation, mostly to document a place, time, or physical condition, and can be a desperate cry for attention.

A Self-Portrait or series can be a form of therapy that allows you to seek a deeper understanding of your inner self. They can help deal with depression, explore feeling powerless or stuck, and capture the sense of illness, grief, or loss from a debilitating injury. They can be quite thought-provoking and transformative. They can also reveal personal change, current functioning, transformation, and well-being over time. In truth, a Self-Portrait is an act of Self-Love and self-honoring, for you are worthy of capturing, admiring, celebrating, and being seen and witnessed.

Self-Portraits are empowering and great markers over time of who you are becoming. They can heal many Self-Woundings and improve many Self-Wonderfuls. Ultimately, a Self-Portrait illustrates the artist of all you are in a creative form.

I am here, a living, breathing, energetic body creating my Self-Portrait at each moment.

I am beautiful inside and out.

I celebrate the creative work of art that I am.

"Self Portraits are a way of revealing something about yourself." –Eric Kandel

"Everything is a self-portrait. A diary. A whole drug history's in a strand of a hair. Your fingernails. The forensic details. The lining of your stomach is a document. The calluses on your hand tell all your secrets. Your teeth give you away. Your accent. The wrinkles around your mouth and eyes. Everything you do shows your hand." –Chuck Palahniuk

"Nature is one of God's self-portraits. You are another." –Martha Beck

MEPSS Activities

Mental – Much of what you believe, honor, think, and value are intangible and can rarely be expressed in a tangible, creative form. Make a list of 12-15 parts of you that represent your values in the deepest sense and reveal who you are at your core. Create a word cloud or cluster* by arranging the words in an image. Change the size of a word to show how important it is to you. Add colors, symbols, shapes, or emojis if you wish. Try using a free online cloud generator to make it easier.

Emotional – Yes, this one asks you to look in a mirror! And it is meant to be fun and spontaneous. In one minute, make various faces that align with your emotions that flow from one to another. For example, go from happy to excited to disappointed to whatever comes to you. Don't think about it; just let it come. Let your body be part of the expression as much as you can. Record your expressions so you can use them later in a Self-Portrait using any creative form you wish.

Physical – Create a Self-Portrait of a 3" x 3" part of your body with its curves, lines, and details. Use an abstract form of expression, such as a 'Zendoodle'*, so it is unrecognizable to anyone but you. Try to convey what is underneath in a way that expresses your truth about that part of your body right now. Send love to it. Send it appreciation for all it does, even if you don't feel it has a significant role in your well-being or everyday life functioning. Sign it. Claim it as uniquely yours!

Social – Find a photo, magazine picture, or online image that portrays your everyday participation with other people. Trace the image onto a piece of paper by placing it against your lit computer screen or a window. Then turn it over so it becomes the mirror image of the scene. On the mirror image side of the paper, highlight the image with markers, paints, pen, pencil, or the drawing instrument of your choice. Then choose a different way of drawing to contrast with the others in the picture so that they are more subtle and let the image stand out. Frame it and hang it somewhere in your house to remind you that you see the world from your own unique perspective.

Spiritual – Take a walk in nature. Find an object that represents you as your Self-Portrait. Spend time with it, absorbing its energy, ambiance, and meaning. Take a picture of it or take it with you if you can. Put the picture or object in a place where you can regularly reflect and meditate on it and contemplate the deep and timeless qualities you share with nature and the universe.

Self-Portrait

Self-Possession

Self-Possession is the gift of keeping all the puzzle pieces of you together calmly and confidently when under stress.

Self-Possession means owning your presence by being intentional with your choices, how you show up with the energy you bring into the space with your thoughts and words and taking 100% responsibility for your decisions. Even under stress, you have a presence of mind that is calm, cool, collected, composed, confident, charming, and in control. You are deliberate, focused, and intentional.

When you live in a state of Self-Possession, you know your responses to situations and can do what you need to do to stay present in the moment. You can express emotions and feelings without becoming them or letting them overwhelm you. Even in difficult and stressful times, you have grace and poise that guides you through, even if you need to collapse or fall apart later in a safe, private place. You present yourself with your own personal sensibility and style that compliments all your gifts, talents, and skills.

Self-Possession is a great goal. It can free you from the beliefs, shame, and stories that hold you back. You do not need to apologize for who and what you are because you are secure with yourself and others. You can stop denying your desires and take responsibility for them in a focused, innovative, responsible, and unapologetic way. You give your all because you have standards of excellence but don't push for perfection because you know what you are capable and not capable of doing.

Others can rely on you and trust your level-headed insights, decisions, and care. You easily ask for help from others and respond with appreciation. You can easily make decisions because you know what you want and how to move forward to make them happen. You can choose the people you want in your life, those who want to be with you and like you for who you truly are. You trust your intuition and the greater forces at play in the universe. You are willing to take risks, not be attached to a specific outcome, and see the value of letting go in trust and faith of what is.

Self-Possession, along with other Self-Wonderfuls such as Self-Assurance, Self-Confidence, Self-Love, Self-Preservation, and Self-Worth, works together to bring a bit of sassy rebelliousness to all the puzzle pieces that make up Self-Possession.

I remain calm, cool, collected, and in control of myself.

I accept all of who I am and what is present right now.

I own every part of myself and give myself permission to be fully me.

"The greatest possession is self-possession." –Ethyl Watts Munford

"Self-possession is the ability to face without fear life in all its contradictions." –Vivian Gornick

"The posture of a woman who had stood in a casual spotlight in every room she'd ever been in, not for gloss or perfection, for self-possession. Everything she touched she added an apostrophe to." –Stephanie Danler

MEPSS Activities

Mental – Make a list of 3 decisions you regret making. Why do you regret them? What did you learn from them? What would you do differently next time to make better decisions?

Emotional – Bring to mind a person you blamed for something that happened to you. What do you blame them for? Now take your power back as you own the part you played with each person or situation, even if it was only 10%. What does this new sense of power feel like? How will you use it more often?

Physical – Your external appearance reflects your inner aesthetic and comfort with yourself. List 10 pieces of clothing or accessories that express who you are with a healthy sense of pride and Self-Possession. What do you like about each piece, and how does each one give you that feeling of something extra and powerful? What one new accessory might enable you to add to your sense of Self-Possession? Go out and buy it or save up the money to buy it soon.

Social – When you stand strongly in your sense of Self-Possession, you can be a powerful presence for social reform. What social cause or area are you concerned about? What organization might you learn more about and get involved with? What might be the first or next step to work toward a remedy or solution?

Spiritual – Self-Possession does not mean manifesting things on your own. Rather, it calls you to be honest about what you want so the Divine* can begin bringing the best to you. What do you want to show up in the next 3 months for you? 6 months? 1 year? 5 years? 10 Years? Ask with an attitude of appreciation, expectation, and trust, then, guided by your connection to the spiritual energetic realm and your intuition, take a first action step that feels right today, followed by the next and the next until it happens! And make sure you are 100% full of Self-Possession at every moment!

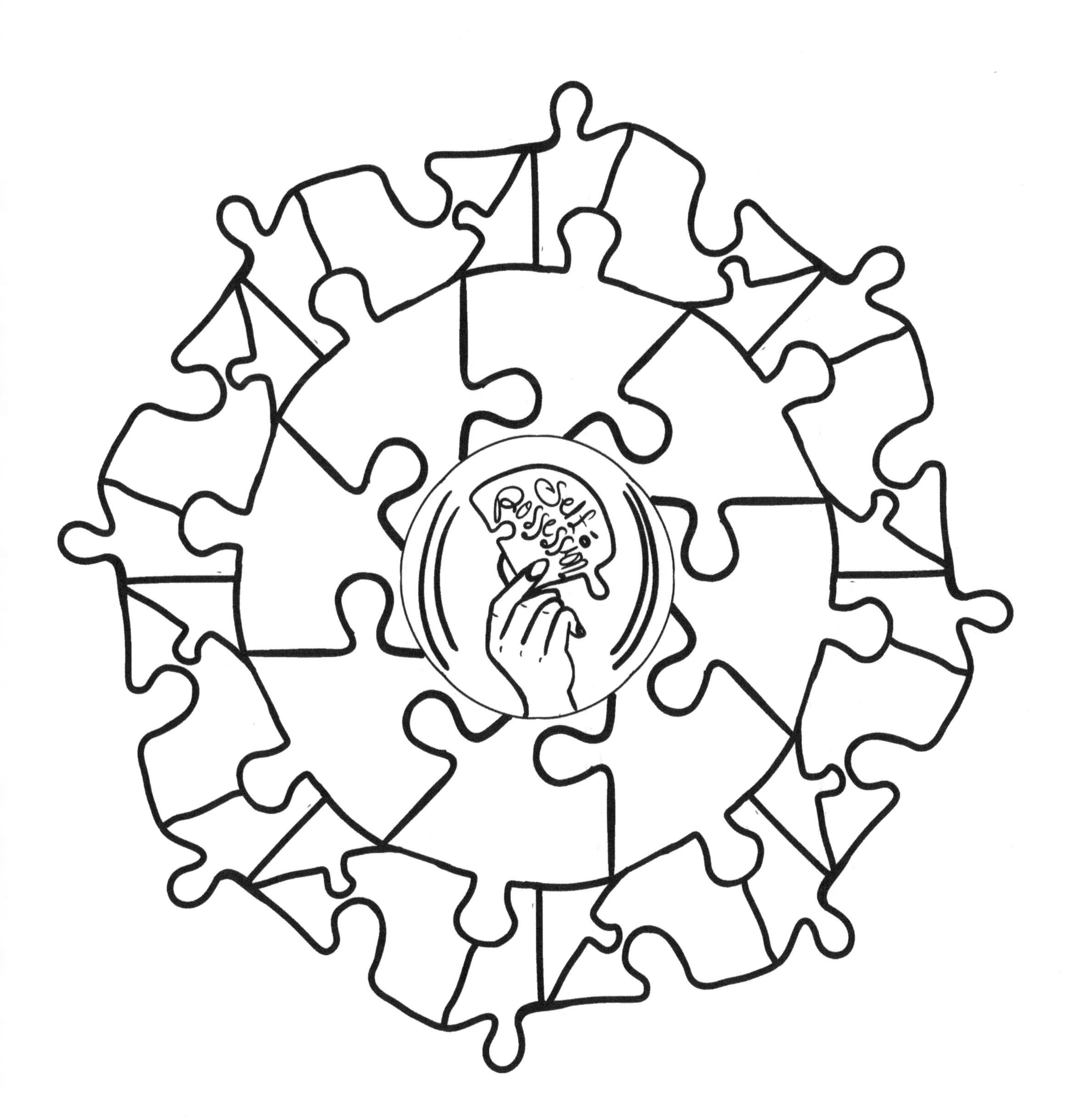
Self-
Possession

Self-Preservation

Self-Preservation is the gift of a life preserver you toss yourself first to ensure you stay alive and healthy to enjoy a productive and satisfying life.

Self-Preservation is the strongest instinctual and practiced act to physically protect yourself from danger, destruction, and harm to ensure your survival. It is also a key element in preserving your mental, emotional, social, and spiritual well-being and growth.

The act of Self-Preservation not only keeps you alive but also energizes, grows, leads, manages, maintains, motivates, and propels your behaviors, personality, and the values by which you choose to live your life from. It makes you the person you are and ensures your existence at each moment in life.

Self-Preservation is one of the most important gifts you can give yourself moment by moment through life. For when you know yourself intimately by honoring your abilities, commitments, desires, gifts, limitations, needs, skills, and talents, and make time to heal, reassess, recover, and savor all that life has to offer, you will continually stoke the energy you need to remain strong in preserving your power and purpose and be faithful to the profound love you show yourself as you act from a place of Self-Preservation.

Self-Preservation covers many things, some of which you may not associate with self-preservation initially. Self-Preservation is akin to another one of the Self-Wonderfuls, Self-Care, for there is no point in caring for yourself if you don't protect your very self you care for. It also relates to many other Self-Wonderfuls such as Self-Appreciation, Self-Control, Self-Determination, Self-Development, Self-Discipline, Self-Empowerment, Self-Esteem, Self-Love, Self-Regard, and Self-Respect.

Often Self-Preservation takes a lower priority than other things in your life, such as education, career, family, friends, health, well-being, entertainment, hobbies, and other responsibilities and commitments that keep you busy, preoccupied, and perhaps overwhelmed. It is important to nurture your whole being and foster your gifts, talents, and skills. It's important to notice your progress or lack thereof and stay on track toward your dreams, goals, and vision for your future. You can also develop ways to check and re-evaluate your progress, noting the changes that support or interfere with where you want to flourish in life. It also calls you to seek assistance and support when you begin to doubt and disparage yourself.

Remember this: Self-Preservation begins and ends with you. You must not only believe in yourself but throw yourself the life preserver to stay alive and healthy and lead a productive and satisfying life.

I know how to protect and preserve myself.

I set the boundaries I need for self-preservation.

I trust my instinct for self-preservation at all times.

"The first law of nature is self-preservation. Cut off that which may harm you. But if it is worth preserving, and is meaningful, nourish it and have no regrets. Ultimately, this is true living and love of self...from within." –T.F. Hodge

"Hunger, love, pain, fear are some of those inner forces which rule the individual's instinct for self-preservation." –Albert Einstein

"Caring for myself is not self-indulgence, it is self-preservation, and that is an act of political warfare." –Audre Lorde

MEPSS Activities

Mental – When and how do you check out? How does this help your Self-Preservation? When might it harm your Self-Preservation, and what might you opt to do instead?

Emotional – Sometimes, you can be in what seems to be or truly is a fight for your life. How might humor bring some emotional relief when things get heavy, stressful, terrifying, and traumatic? What attitudes, behaviors, body or facial expressions, games, jokes, lyrics, people, phrases, pictures, riddles, or stories might ease what you are going through? Choose one and do it now!

Physical – Your body is the only one you have. Make a list of 10 ways your body supports you daily. Offer a gesture of appreciation for each one. Now, pick 2 things you can commit to work on to improve your health, energy, and stamina, so your body can be your best ally in life. What will be your first step in each one? Do it!

Social – Review your day and week and list how other groups, institutions, and organizations assist and support your safety and Self-Preservation in your life, relationships, and work. Then create a gesture of thanks for one of them and give it to them. Be creative, and if you can, let the gesture reflect what you have received from them. If you liked doing it for one, you might consider making this a regular activity.

Spiritual – Recall a time or two when fear was the instinct or motive for Self-Preservation rather than loving protection and care. What were the consequences or results coming from fear? What was the story you told yourself about it? Now recall a time or two when Self-Preservation came from out of nowhere or synchronicity had its role in Self-Preservation. How did that feel? What was your reaction or response to that? What was the story you told yourself (or shared with others) about it? Find a small token to remind you of this supportive Self-Preservation incident and keep it somewhere you can see it often to remind you of the power beyond you that loves, assists, and supports you at all times.

Self-
Preservation

Self-Reflection

Self-Reflection is the gift of time taken looking into a mirror to inventory, evaluate, and understand yourself in order to become more truly you.

Self-Reflection brings perspective to your life. It helps you learn, grow, appreciate, and understand yourself in new and deepening ways. It goes deeper below the surface of what you think, feel, and sense daily, allowing you to retain every aspect of an experience or decision. It clarifies your thinking, allowing you to focus on what matters to you and why.

Practicing Self-Reflection requires taking a 'time out' from your fast-paced everyday life and pausing to ponder yourself. It is an intentional pause or stop that requires discipline and being gentle with yourself to master. It is an essential skill that increases inner peace because you are deeply connected to your true self.

Practicing Self-Reflection has many benefits and makes the challenge of taking the time well worth it. It allows you to gain perspective and see where thoughts, emotions, and feelings cloud your judgment and cause you to lose sight of what truly matters. It allows you to process events and achieve clarity on them. It helps you respond more effectively in conversations and relationships. It helps you consider the consequences of your words and actions and not repeat the same mistakes over and over again. It helps you listen and learn about yourself, face your shadows, and understand more about yourself so you can live a healthy, balanced, and integrated life.

When you fail to reflect on your life, you lose perspective, lose sight of the things that matter most to you, and get sidetracked. If you can't identify when you have acted regrettably, you will likely act that way again. This may prolong the ill feelings and tension you have with a colleague, family member, or friend and could usher in potential long-term ramifications that significantly erode the relationship. Without 'course corrections' along the way, you will feel out of control of your life and experience continual setbacks.

Self-Reflection creates freedom to be more yourself. It lets you see what you need to work on and what is going well. It develops at least 4 other Self-Wonderfuls: Self-Acceptance, Self-Awareness, Self-Confidence, and Self-Compassion.

Self-Reflection allows you to have a greater connection with yourself and to live a healthy, happy, and wholehearted life. Use the gift of time to reflect by looking in a mirror to inventory, evaluate, and understand yourself in order to become more truly you.

I give myself permission to take time out to reflect.

I make time to be quiet and reflect on my life's lessons and blessings.

I look back and am thankful for the lessons I have learned and the growth that resulted.

"People who have had little self-reflection live life in a huge reality blind spot." –Bryant McGill

"...Until you take the journey of self-reflection, it is almost impossible to grow or learn in life." –Iyanla Vanzant

"Difficulty creates the opportunity for self-reflection and compassion." –Suzan-Lori Parks

MEPSS Activities

Mental – Develop your 'inner witness' by noticing your thoughts like passing clouds*. When one, in particular, attracts your attention, pull it down in front of you and simply let it be there. Ask it – how did this thought arise? What came before it? What sensations and emotions came with it? What does it want me to know? What does it want me to do, if anything? Honor the wisdom that this thought has given you in some simple way.

Emotional – Develop your 'inner witness' by noticing an emotion or feeling in your heart area. Allow it to develop fully without attaching any thoughts or stories to it. Just let it be. As it seems to begin to wane, ask it, 'What are you connected to? What is your gift to me? What further reflection needs to take place?' Spend time until you have fully felt it, and it subsides and disappears.

Physical – Take an inventory of what you ate, how much you ate, when you ate, where you ate, whom you ate it with, and why. Then write down the answers to these questions: Why did you choose what you ate? How did you feel when you ate it? How did you feel 2 hours afterward? What kinds of bodily responses did you experience? Why did you eat where you did? How did eating with others or alone affect your food consumption? Why did you eat in the first place? What did you learn about yourself after answering and reflecting on these questions?

Social – Take time today to reflect on how much you have. It may not be all you want, but remember, someone somewhere dreams of having what you have. Now reflect on how you might offer someone dreaming of having one of what you have and donate to a cause or organization to make that dream a reality.

Spiritual – Contemplation is the spiritual practice of being fully present in the open and receptive in the heart-knowing space in order to listen deeply and better connect with yourself and Divine love. It is how you can work out the experiences that words can't express, learn from them, and bravely allow yourself to be transformed by them, even when your normal mode of thinking can't make sense of them. You can do this by focusing on your breathing, repeating a chosen word that has spiritual meaning for you, moving (yoga or dancing), or music (drumming, singing, or chanting). Through contemplation and life, the Divine works on us slowly and secretly. Contemplative practices gradually rewire our brains to perceive and respond to reality with love. Begin with 5 minutes and work up to 20 minutes. When you finish, stand in front of a full-length mirror, look at your reflection, and sense yourself in the present moment.

Self-Reflection

Self-Regard

Self-Regard is accepting with open arms the gift of all parts of you while respecting those parts that tend to shy away from your embrace.

Self-Regard is the ability to accept and respect yourself, appreciating all parts of you regardless of how you rate them. It is about being genuine as yourself, even as you experience the ups and downs of life. In fact, regardless of what happens, you feel good about yourself, are in touch with the here and now, and are continually changing and growing on your way to meeting your dreams and goals.

Because you have healthy Self-Regard for yourself, you have no trouble acknowledging when you have made mistakes, been wrong, or didn't know all the answers. You use these situations to learn more about yourself, practice new ways to enhance further growth and move closer to living your best life. You adopt an 'I can do this' spirit and believe in yourself.

When your Self-Regard is low, you tend to doubt your abilities, be hard on yourself, blame others for your mistakes, second-guess your decisions, hurt, discredit, or put down other people, and hold back from taking acting confidently and leading others, all the while inflating yourself to prove your worth.

Carl Rogers* made an important contribution to psychology when he introduced the concept of 'unconditional positive regard,'* concluding that you need a supportive environment to fulfill your potential. Of course, this is an ideal, and yet, the more you can practice unconditional positive regard for yourself, the more you will be open and accepting of all experiences; avoid judging and preconceptions; fully appreciate the present moment; think creatively; trust your feelings, instincts, intuition, and decisions; feel congruent with all parts of you; and be satisfied and happy with life.

Self-Regard is respecting yourself as a human being who can choose who and what you want to be, how you will make those choices, and what those choices will offer you over your lifetime. So, accept with open arms your overflowing pile of gifts of all parts of you, even those parts that tend to shy away from your embrace.

I celebrate everything I am!

I believe in my ability to become who I am meant to be.

I treat myself with unconditional positive Self-Regard in every moment.

"If I give more to myself, I can ask more from myself. Self-regard isn't selfish." –Gretchen Rubin

"Love in the form of longing and deprivation lowers the self-regard." –Sigmund Freud

'Having a low opinion of yourself is not 'modesty.' It's self-destruction. Holding your uniqueness in high (self)-regard is not 'egotism.' It's a necessary precondition to happiness and success.' –Bobbe Sommer

MEPSS Activities

Mental – Using one sticky note for each, make simple affirming sentences of 30 qualities that make up the unique you. Use sentence starters such as, 'I am __________', 'I am able to __________', 'I can______', 'I am good at ________' and 'I am proud of _______". Then use one each morning for a month as an affirmation you say to yourself as you look in the mirror. Then repeat them the next month and the next until you truly believe these statements.

Emotional – List 10 healthy and 10 unhealthy feelings you have about yourself and how each affects you. Choose one a day from each list (with a one-day break in between) to focus on this week to make you feel better about yourself.

Physical – OK, you have permission to go all out and compare yourself with all the fake and false magazine images you can find. Compare your physical features, mental capacity, emotional reactions, and feelings to what others feel in the expressive arts, movies, music, poetry, and stories. Compare your career trajectory, current job, the number of true friends, and the number of social media likes. Compare your spiritual qualities and practices; compare away! What did you discover about yourself? How did it make you feel to compare and compare and compare? Now be honest and realistic and state what is true about you. Offer yourself unconditional positive Self-Regard and throw yourself some kind of celebration to celebrate the amazing and Simply Self-Wonderful, perfectly imperfect person you are!

Social – There is often a vast difference between how you see yourself and how others see you. Validate your self-perception by asking others you love, care, and can be honest with you, to offer feedback about yourself. How is your perception similar? How is your perception different? Is there something that stands out that would be beneficial for you to consider changing or improving upon? Choose one small action to take and see where it leads you.

Spiritual – Practice being as accepting and forgiving of yourself as you are of others by finding a photo of yourself as a young child. Look into the eyes of your young self and offer yourself unconditional acceptance, love, and positive regard. What happened to you as a young child that caused you to stop regarding yourself as a perfectly imperfect beloved child of the Divine*? Offer forgiveness* to your current self and make any amends you need to complete it. Give yourself a hug as often as you remember to!

Self-Regard

Self-Reliance

Self-Reliance is the gift of having yourself on speed dial to come to your aid at any time.

Self-Reliance is relying on your own powers, judgments, and resources rather than those of others to make decisions about your life. It is finding the determination and strength within yourself to do something despite the difficulties and challenges that may be present. It implies a sense of boldness, independence, and freedom to claim your abilities, skills, and talents to make your life what you wish it to be and find contentment.

Self-Reliance requires you to think independently, trust your own instincts, and know in the deepest sense who you are. It calls you to embrace your individuality, accept yourself completely, and find your greatest happiness within yourself. It allows you to listen to yourself in a crowd and stand up for what you believe, even if you know it may be dismissed or rejected. It motivates you to take steps toward achieving your goals and being willing to take chances that might inhibit someone else.

Self-Reliance breeds an inner confidence that allows you to appreciate and accept your unique gifts, character strengths, and achievements and realize your dreams and goals. Self-Reliance is empowering and enables you to refuse anything that would force you to conform without your full consent. It brings inner peace knowing that your happiness comes from you and that others' disapproval reflects their own unhappiness and judgment. Self-Reliance allows you to step into your greatness and is a courageous way to live your life.

Self-Reliance also shapes your relationships and how you treat the requests and demands of others. It helps you establish emotional intelligence, develop healthy emotional boundaries, and not take on other people's expectations or emotional energy. It gives you perspective, which in turn gives you direction and purpose.

Some may say that being too Self-Reliant can destroy your relationships, put too much pressure on you, and keep you independent to the point of isolation. This is the double-edged sword of Self-Reliance. On the one hand, being independent, self-sufficient, and resilient is wonderful. But when you do everything for yourself, you may end up depriving yourself of true love, commitment, trust, and the pleasure others have when they can be of service. The key is to develop an interdependence in relationships so that they remain beneficial and appropriate for others and you.

With Self-Reliance, you can be true to yourself, make your own decisions, accept the price of your actions, trust yourself, stick to your path no matter how tough it gets, engage the world on your terms, not the world's, and be the answer at the other end of your own speed dial.

I am self-reliant, creative, and persistent in whatever I do.

I am fully capable and committed to achieving my goals.

I balance self-reliance with help from others.

"Freedom comes from strength and self-reliance."
–Lisa Murkowski

'Self-reliance is the key to a vigorous life. One must look inward to find their own answers.' –Robin Williams

"The difficulties, hardships, and trials of life, the obstacles... are positive blessings. They knit the muscles more firmly and teach self-reliance. –William Matthews

MEPSS Activities

Mental – You cannot change the external events, challenges, pressures, or stressors that arise around you, but you do have control over how you see and react to them.

You can plan ahead by learning from past experiences and choosing more helpful, new strategies to cope with them. One way is to train yourself to think more optimistically and find the positive in every situation. Choose a recent past situation to reflect on where things got out of control. Ask yourself, 'What thought took me to overwhelm, panic, or shutdown? Where did that thought take me? And that thought?' Continue along the thought chain until you can't go any farther. Now ask yourself, 'What new thought will help me shift into a more positive, flexible mindset and help me be more in control?' Then follow that thought to the next one and the next one. Use visualization to imagine yourself making that new thought response to the original situation. What are the new outcomes?

Emotional – Practicing EFT – Emotional Freedom Technique* or 'Tapping' can help you learn how to regulate your emotions in a healthy way so you can be impartial and objective when challenging situations arise. Tap the pattern and breathe slowly in and out to initiate a calm and centered state of being. Use the mantra 'in spite of the fact that I have this issue, I am OK. I accept myself.' At the end of the sequence, give yourself a big loving hug!

Physical – What difficulty, hardship, illness, obstacle, or trial has contributed to your Self-Reliance? Spend a few minutes noting the qualities and what they have given you that you may not have acquired any other way. Then offer gratitude for each of them.

Social – Becoming aware of when you tend to turn to others is part of learning to practice Self-Reliance. Make a list of things that you regularly ask others for. Now choose one and set a goal of accomplishing it on your own. When you do, celebrate the sense of accomplishment, the gift of a greater belief in your own abilities, and in doing something new for yourself!

Spiritual – What is your Self-Reliance superpower? What is one thing that makes you who you are? Draw a cartoon or caricature of yourself with your creative superpower of the universe and sign your name to it. Or, if drawing isn't your thing, use a computer application or have someone create one for you.

Self-Reliance
1
2
3
4
5
6
7
8
9
0
#
*

Self-Respect

Self-Respect is the gift of a book of etiquette you use to treat yourself with courtesy as your most important and honored guest.

Self-Respect is an 'inside job,' a deep inner sense you have about yourself that no one can offer you but you. It comes from loving yourself and having a sense of honor and dignity about yourself, your choices, and your life. You feel good about yourself, value your abilities, attributes, skills, and talents, and can also accept your flaws and failings. Self-Respect motivates you to live a life of authenticity and personal integrity, making choices regardless of what anyone else thinks of you. Self-Respect is being the kind of person you are satisfied with, showing the world, and being someone you and the people you care about are proud of.

Self-Respect isn't limited to how you feel about yourself. Self-Respect builds your character and gives you control over your choices in attitudes, behaviors, beliefs, career path, relationships, situations, values, and anything else that defines you as uniquely you. Self-Respect is vital for maintaining a healthy self-image and allows you to feel confident in every situation and accepting of the person you are and are becoming. It is about knowing and valuing your worth above all else and standing up for yourself when you are being treated in a manner that diminishes and disparages you.

Self-Respect takes into account that not everyone will respect you or treat you well, which is absolutely fine because you know deep within yourself that you do not need anyone else's approval to be who you are. You are you, and you respect yourself for that. Self-Respect allows you to adjust your life and remove the circumstances, people, and situations that you are tolerating who treat you with anger, disrespect, unfairness, seek to harm or lie to you. It gives you the power of refusal not to stoop to another's level but to treat them with the respect they have naturally as a human being.

If you are Self-Respectful, you will have no need for comparisons or jealousy when others shine in the spotlight. You respect the people who care about you and are humble and wise enough to realize that they may have valuable advice and wisdom to offer you and want what's best for you and that it is always your choice to receive or reject it.

Self-Respect is the gift of a book of etiquette you use to treat yourself with courtesy as your most honored guest. And it allows you to respect others as the honored guests they are.

I honor and respect myself.

I choose to live a life of authenticity and personal integrity.

I walk away from disrespectful people and situations.

"If we lose love and self-respect for each other, this is how we finally die." –Maya Angelou

"The willingness to accept responsibility for one's own life is the source from which self-respect springs." –Joan Didion

"They will call you arrogant for having self-respect." –Thibaut

MEPSS Activities

Mental – Often, you apologize when there is no need to unless you've made a genuine mistake. List 20 occasions where you have said 'sorry' as a habit to fill the space as a response. Which ones called for an apology, and which were cases where you did not stand up and respect the wonderful person you are? Pick 5 and write more empowering responses you might make instead.

Emotional – Write your own book of etiquette to use to treat yourself with courtesy as your most important and honored guest. What 20 rules or guidelines are important or necessary for your internal gratification and satisfaction? If you want, you can illustrate it with drawings, pictures, symbols, or words. Be creative and have fun with this! It might not even take the shape of a typical book! What did you discover about yourself, and which 3 will you practice?

Physical – No one can make you feel bad about yourself without your permission. So, embrace your lifestyle choices and decisions you've made throughout your life. List 25 things, such as length of hair, dress style, type of food and diet you adhere to, partner, child, and family choices, career, where to live, type of home, etc. All those choices are yours alone. Together they make up who you are. Which ones have changed over the years? Why? Which ones have pretty much stayed the same? Why? How have they helped your Self-Respect? Which ones hindered your Self-Respect? Are there any you want to change now? What first step will you take to change?

Social – If you always say yes to people who ask you to do something without giving anything in return, then you may need to build your own no boundaries* of Self-Respect. Picture a doormat or make a simple one with a piece of cardboard. List 10 things that people try to lay at your feet, then give into their pleading, and let them walk all over you even though you don't want to or resent accepting. What keeps you acting like a doormat? Why is it so hard to say no? What action will show them that you mean no next time? What phrase will help you say no when this happens next time?

Spiritual – Draw a simple rainbow big enough to write words on, using colored pencils, markers, pastels, or watercolor paint on an 8.5 x 11-inch piece of paper. Start with red, then orange, yellow, green, blue, and violet. Write the qualities you are proudest of and that are helping you reach your dreams on each color of the rainbow. Having pride in yourself is a key aspect of Self-Respect. Frame the picture, then hang it in a prominent place where you can look at it often.

Self-
Respect

Self-Starter

Self-Starter is the gift of a 'can do' attitude that you give yourself to seize new opportunities and achieve the goals you have for yourself.

A Self-Starter is a person who takes the initiative, is motivated, ambitious, confident, enthusiastic, loyal, motivated, has a vision and particular goals to meet that vision. If you are a Self-Starter, you like new challenges, taking risks, solving problems, achieving goals, and easily working without supervision. You have expectations and commonly trust your intuition, embrace challenges, are comfortable with discomfort, set high expectations, and create successful outcomes.

As a Self-Starter you often take a 'hands-on' approach in your home and professional life. You begin projects independently, easily, and often. You are proactive rather than reactive and easily take charge of situations. You create a plan, work hard, and don't mind the hard work, knowing it will take you to your goal. You assume a leadership role, know how to move past difficulties, and find alternative solutions to accomplish your goal.

You are disciplined and organized, and when you get distracted or tempted to lose focus, you dig deep inside to rekindle the inner drive that propels you forward. You recognize the value of short-term sacrifice for long-term reward. Learning and improving, knowing that things could always improve, propels you with purposeful energy.

Even though a Self-Starter works independently and is often the pioneer of a project or goal, you rely on the aid and assistance of others to get things done. You have good communication skills and can articulate ideas, desires, and goals to others that help them see why they are important or interesting. You are a great networker and can influence others and demonstrate the value of what you are attempting to create. You handle criticism and rejection well, filter out insignificant opinions, and focus on goals and ambitions. You will take some of these to heart to learn and grow personally from them.

Being a Self-Starter takes courage, knowing there are uncertainties and risks of failure. But instead of letting fear of failure prevent you from trying or taking over, you see failures as opportunities for learning and growth.

The good news is that you don't have to be born a Self-Starter, and it's never too late to become one. You can start to learn by building these traits within yourself right now by acting from that 'can-do' attitude to help you reach your goals.

I am capable of creating anything I want in life.

I act from a 'can do' attitude and easily reach my goals.

I am capable, committed, confident, consistent, courageous, and clear about what I want to create with each opportunity for success.

"Most of us are not pure self-starters; most people need role models, they need coaches, they need exemplars, they may need some discipline or some rewards. We need to be motivated." –Tyler Cowen

"Be a self-starter. Let your first hour set the theme for success and positive action that is certain to echo through your entire day. Today will never happen again. Don't waste it with a false start or no start at all. You were not born to fail." –Og Mandimo

"Be a self-starter. Do it now! When you don't know how to do something, start. Beware of the paralysis of analysis. Be a person of action." –Mamie McCullough

MEPSS Activities

Mental – Rather than using a lot of mental energy, stressing your brain, and tiring it, let the other two intelligence centers help. Choose a situation you need to clarify. Relax your mind and drop down into your heart and notice the information offered to you from your heart. Now, relax even more and drop down into your body, listen to your gut instinct. Notice sensations and locations in various body parts and ask each of them, 'What do you want to tell me?' Now take the information from all three areas, mind, heart, and body, and synthesize it into the information and solutions you need.

Emotional – Even though you are determined not to let your fear dictate your actions, you are still human and feel afraid like everyone else. Make friends with your fear. Write a 'Dear Fear' letter and thank it for the power and courage it brings you and anything else you want to thank it for.

Physical – Self-Starters are often in continuous action, feel like work is never done, and find it hard to slow down, relax, and give your body a break. List 25 ways to relax, some on the spot for just a few moments or minutes, others for an hour or two, and others for a day, weekend, or week.

Social – Excellent communication skills are a must for everyone, especially for Self-Starters who work with others regularly. Review the phrases you use to encourage others and what the responses are from the receiver of your encouragement. Review the phrases you used without thinking that harmed or unsettled the receiver. Work on a list of new phrases and rephrases to uplift, encourage, and honor the person's value and worth.

Spiritual – Determining to accomplish great things with your life and make the world a better place for all propels your action toward deeply meaningful goals for the world. Now is the time to dream. What qualities do you envision for the world's future, and which 3 will you actively work toward? Find or make a symbol to challenge you forward and keep it visible for encouragement and motivation.

Self-Starter

Self-Trust

Self-Trust is the resourceful, reliable inner gift of a firm grip that holds your own hand, knowing you have what it takes to survive and make your way in the world.

Self-Trust is a skill you learn to rely on your own inner resources to navigate your life and the world. You make a choice each moment, using your mental, emotional, intuitive, and physical abilities and resources. Self-Trust is a kind of independence where you keep commitments and promises for yourself.

Self-Trust is not arrogance. Self-Trust is becoming your own best friend and maintaining that relationship through the ups and downs of your life. The only person you know you can count on is yourself. You are the only one that can be consistently supportive, kind, and loving to yourself. Self-Trust means that you can take care of your own needs and safety and refuse to give up on yourself.

Other components of Self-Trust include being your authentic self, being aware of your emotions, feelings, and thoughts and expressing them appropriately, building on your strengths, following through with things you've committed to, helping yourself out in a time of need, keeping your word to yourself, knowing when you need to care for yourself first, knowing you can survive mistakes and try again, pursuing what you want without being limited or stopped by others, and respecting your own opinion. On top of this, Self-Trust is a precursor to both creativity and intuition and allows you to create the life you want for yourself to more than survive in the world but thrive and flourish!

Self-Trust can be lost and restored many times over your lifetime. Your truth may have been discounted by family, friends, groups, or society, leaving you insecure and doubtful. Then again, you may have gone against your own heart because your truth was inconvenient to speak at the time, and you could not stand up for yourself. Many Self-Woundings weaken your Self-Trust. It takes practice to strengthen and feel more confident and trusting in yourself. You won't always trust yourself to do or say the right things, make the right decision, follow every rule, or be perfect. But it means you have the mindset that whatever comes your way, you can handle it. You trust yourself enough to do it and overcome a failure, mistake, or slip-up and survive. You use the resourceful, reliable inner gift of a firm grip that holds your own hand, knowing you have what it takes to survive and make your way in the world.

I trust myself completely.
It is safe for me to trust myself.
I trust myself to make the right decision.

"The process of building trust is an interesting one, but it begins with yourself, with what I call self-trust, and with your own credibility, your own trustworthiness. If you think about it, it's hard to establish trust with others if you can't trust yourself." –Steven Covey

"Our self-trust is such a subtle thing that it still comes around whispering to us even after we are sure it is gone." –Aiden Wilson Tozer

"So, remember these two things: you are talented, and you are original. Be sure of that. I say this because self-trust is one of the very most important things in writing." –Brenda Ueland

MEPSS Activities.

Mental – Read *Autobiography in Five Short Chapters* by Portia Nelson*. Then, recall a time when you made it through a tough time. How did you get through it? List 20 things you did and use them to write your autobiography in five short chapters. Have fun and notice the self-trust that builds as you creatively write your autobiography.

Emotional – Be your own researcher and 'study' your relationship with yourself. What are you saying to yourself? What are your emotions and feelings saying to you? What is your body saying to you? What is your intuition saying to you? Listen to them and describe 10 things you learned from this 'study.' What 3 commitments will you make to maintain a good relationship with yourself? Choose one and take the first step to make it real.

Physical – Creativity comes from Self-Trust. You trust your instincts and allow them an expressive outlet. Gather a few creative materials or art supplies and make something. Instead of paying attention to what you are creating, pay attention to what your body is doing. What are your body's rhythms with regard to creating? Is there a change in energy intensity, flow, pauses, and various speeds? What are the thoughts, emotions, and sensations occurring in your body? What other ideas, images, memories, pictures, and stories come to mind and either stay or float away? Where does your creativity come from? Reflect on how this compares to getting your best work done, having creative and flow moments in your day, and expressing yourself authentically and freely. What does it tell you about Self-Trust?

Social – What is your song—the song you sing (or want to sing) for everyone to hear? Write 5 simple verses of the song about your unique energy, gifts, influence, opinions, passions, power, presence, risks, strengths, talents, and values you are sharing within the world just by being you and trusting yourself. You can use a familiar tune or make up one yourself. Record yourself singing it and sharing it with others on social media if you dare.

Spiritual – What do you make of the premise that 'if you are here, the authorities of the universe put you here for some task strictly appointed for you'? Who are the 'authorities of the universe' for you? What task do you feel strictly appointed to? How are you working to bring it into the world? If you don't have answers to these questions, spend some time in silence and reflection. What was revealed? How will you follow your inner guidance in the coming week?

SELF-TRUST

Self-Understanding

Self-Understanding is the gift of reading the textbook of you and getting a 100% A grade.

Self-Understanding is objectively knowing who you are from the inside out and what led you to become who you are. It's the grand view of your life that goes beyond all the small choices and differences that people use in comparison. Self-Understanding celebrates, honors, and rejoices in your uniqueness in all its many forms. It's about what matters most to you, makes you come alive, focuses your energy, feeds your heart and soul, and shows what drains your energy and spirit. Amazing things will happen when you express who you were meant to be! You will be yourself without anyone else's permission!

Self-Understanding is a process. It's something you must do that can't be done simply by growing up and growing old! It's a willingness to answer the call and be led on an unpredictable journey to explore whatever comes. Self-Understanding brings you face-to-face with your abilities, actions, behaviors, beliefs, body, choices, conflict style, desires, dislikes, doubts, dreams, eccentricities, embarrassments, emotions, feelings, frustrations, idiosyncrasies, insecurities, intentions, interests, limitations, mistakes, moods, morals, passions, personal rhythms, personality, preferences, principles, purpose, relationships, strengths, temperament, thoughts, tolerances, values, and weaknesses; all the things that you need to become the authentic, Self-Actualized, Simply Self-Wonderful You!

Self-Understanding provides you with a sense of purpose for your life. You are confident in who you are, have fewer doubts and fears, know why you are here, know what you can and cannot do, make decisions easier, and feel secure in yourself. Your outside actions are congruent with your feelings, motivations, preferences, and values, and you make better choices. You feel more alive, energized, and excited and have less inner conflict. You have no problem standing up for yourself and easily say 'yes' and 'no' when it is appropriate to maintain your boundaries, integrity, and values. Because you know yourself, your strengths, and weaknesses, you also have compassion, tolerance, and understanding of others. This self-understanding makes everything come easier in life. With Self-Understanding, you are happiest when you express the textbook of your true self in a way that helps you get a 100% A grade!

I understand myself more with every opportunity life offers.

I use all experiences of my life for self-understanding.

The more I understand myself, the more I understand others.

"Self-understanding is a lifetime endeavor. It is not a weekend seminar. It does not come in capsule form." –Vironika Wilde Tugaleva

"To deny our pasts is to burn the bridge we must cross to self-understanding." –Richard Paul Evans

"As a teacher I realize that what one learns in school doesn't serve for very much at all, that the only thing one can really learn is self-understanding and this is something that can't be taught." –Laura Esquivel

MEPSS Activities

Mental – Make a Life Timeline* masterpiece. Review your timeline, and answer these questions to deepen your Self-Understanding: Which events changed you the most? Which helped you grow? Which do you see in a different light now than you did when it occurred? Which memories make you smile with affection? Which memories still give you pangs of pain, regret, or sorrow? Spend time over the week or as long as you wish going deeper until you have an even better Self-Understanding. How would you summarize your life in 6 words?

Emotional – List the 10 top books that impacted your Self-Understanding and who you are becoming. Re-read one, and if you wish, recommend it to someone you care about. Then write a thank-you note to the author about the impact and how it changed your life. If you can, send it to the publisher to give to the author. You can also post the book recommendation and impact on social media or even create a group of friends to read it together and hear how it impacted them. If you want, you can even list all 10! Be creative and have fun!!!

Physical – An addiction is anything you can't stop yourself from doing. It's very important to find the root cause and why you felt the desire or need to misuse a substance or harm yourself in the first place. What can't you stop yourself from doing? What are you trying to alleviate or escape from? What is your first step to getting the help you need? What help might you need to make that first step? Reach out to a mental health professional and get that help today. And if you are already taking the steps you need, celebrate yourself in some way for your determination, perseverance, and success. How has this contributed to your Self-Understanding?

Social – Personality Typing can be very beneficial. Rather than think of it as a way to categorize yourself or others, think of it as a helpful tool to aid in your Self-Understanding and assist your understanding of others so you can have the best relationships possible. Here are 4 to explore: Clifton Strengths Finder*, Enneagram*, MBTI – Myers Briggs Type Indicator*, and VIA (Values in Action) Character Survey*

Spiritual – Meditation is simple but never easy. It involves being in the present moment, and there are many ways to meditate. If you have never tried meditation, do a little research and find a practice that resonates with you. You don't have to sit, sometimes walking allows you to focus better. To begin, focus on your breathing and let your thoughts move through like passing clouds. If you attach a thought to them, simply return to focusing on your breath. Begin with 1 minute and work your way up to 10 minutes. Over time you will notice many benefits. When you notice your progress, make a list of them, and let this encourage you to continue. There is no end or arrival; there is simply the present.

Self-Worth

Self-Worth is the gift of feeling like a billion bucks and knowing you are priceless.

Self-Worth is not about measuring yourself based on external actions such as appearance, net worth, what you do, what you achieve, or who you know. It's about who you are, not what you do. It is about valuing your inherent worth as a human being. Self-Worth is constant and doesn't vary in the moment or the situation.

If you try to search for Self-Worth by constantly comparing yourself to others, you will never feel good about who you are. There will always be someone more attractive, capable, successful, and fill-in-the-blank here. Instead of rating yourself, just be YOU!

You feel unworthy of love, happiness, and success when you lack Self Worth. You feel small, insignificant, unstable, and insecure and have constant anxiety and fear that taints everything like poison. You may try to put on a tough façade or a mask to try and fool others, but deep down, you know it's all a lie. When you lack Self-Worth, an innate sense of dignity is missing.

When you experience low Self-Worth, you struggle! It's hard to be assertive about your needs (if you even know what they are), set boundaries, accept compliments, believe anyone could love you, feel valued, speak up, and share yourself. You put others' needs above your own, settle for less in relationships and jobs, and let others mistreat you, feel depressed and fearful.

We all have that Saboteur voice that evaluates your every move and tells you, 'You are worthless,' which undermines your Self-Worth and leads to various Self-Woundings that make you feel even worse about yourself.

The good news is that you can challenge the Saboteur, stand in your true power, and begin to see yourself for who you truly are. You can appreciate your own desires, feelings, thoughts, and values. You are more accepting and loving of yourself. You create healthy personal boundaries and remove toxic people and habits from your life. You find loving friends and partners and improve the overall quality of your life. You become more curious, make wise decisions, and are open to your experiences by practicing other Self-Wonderfuls such as Self-Respect, Self-Compassion, Self-Esteem, and Self-Confidence rather than continuing the Self-Woundings of Self-Criticism, Self-Deprecation, Self-Doubt, Self-Judgment, and Self-Sabotage and more.

Self-Worth is an inside job! By pursuing activities and practices that are meaningful to you regardless of what others think, as well as acting in line with your own beliefs and values, you can truly develop a sense of your own Self-Worth, find meaning in life, be that valued, beloved person that you truly are, honor that value in your life and achievements, and feel like a million bucks!

I am a unique and special human being.
I feel good about being alive and being me.
I celebrate and rejoice in my uniqueness and worth.

"Your self-worth is determined by you. You don't have to depend on someone to tell you who you are." –Beyoncé Knowles

"True abundance isn't based on our net worth; it's based on our self-worth." –Gabrielle Bernstein

"Self-worth sets the standard that life meets." –Jewel

MEPSS Activities

Mental – To quell the voice of the Saboteur*, take time to write down and examine some of the false ideas you have been taught about yourself. They may be subtle and difficult to untangle, so be patient and give yourself time to just be with the inquiry. If you can, figure out where they came from and correct the idea with a new statement of truth about yourself.

Emotional – Spend 5 minutes writing a list of qualities and characteristics no one can take away from you. Notice how you feel when you own these. Give yourself a gold star (or more than one) for each. Use stickers and place the list on the refrigerator or somewhere you will see it often and smile.

Physical – Scan your body, beginning at the top of your head and going down through your body all the way to your feet. For each body part (you might want to find an anatomical diagram to use), including organs, tissues, glands, and cells, speak a word of thanks for what it enables you to do each day. Then offer it an inner smile. When you finish, give yourself a big hug first with your arms crossed one way, then with your arms crossed the other way. This gives your body, mind, and spirit a burst of endorphins, neurotransmitters that act as your body's natural pain relievers, enhancing your mood too.

Social – Replace your pattern of people pleasing by focusing on a time you changed yourself for the sake of others. What made you do it? What did you give up of yourself? What will you do differently next time a similar situation arises so that you can stand in your full and valuable Self-Worth?

Spiritual – If you died, who would you want to be remembered for as a person of value? Write your obituary and be grateful for the value you offer others and the world. Or write one to aspire to as you keep living your life.

Self-Worth

Selfless

Selfless is the humble gift of strength in your self-importance that has no reason to exaggerate, thus treating others in kindness, generosity, and love in the same way you would treat yourself.

Selfless is the opposite of Selfish. It means you think less of yourself and more about others. Another similar word is altruism which means you choose others' welfare over your own advantages. Being Selfless is a key to fulfillment and happiness, especially in relationships, social connections, health, well-being, and living longer. This may appear contrary at first, yet, when you act in a Selfless manner, it may ultimately indirectly benefit you either at the time or later.

When you act from a Selfless place, you are concerned about the well-being of others, have something to offer, and want to offer it. You appear so down to earth that you have an instinct to put others' needs first and treat them the way you would treat yourself, with no sense of increased self-importance. You are caring, compassionate, humble, and generous not just to your fellow humans but to all creatures and the earth itself. You consider and deliberate how your actions and decisions will affect others and choose the best options for all involved. You don't dominate a conversation but rather enjoy taking time to listen and understand others. You rarely discuss your problems to prevent others from worrying about them. You love to serve and volunteer, knowing that small acts of kindness and larger ones can provide long-lasting happiness. You find joy in others' successes as well as your own.

Being Selfless is contrary to normal behavior because you usually help others to feel good about yourself. And you expect something in return. When you offer Selfless service, it must be voluntary and undertaken for the right reasons with no ulterior motives; otherwise, the pressure to be of service negates the promise of its rewards. This leads to 'keeping score,' obligation, and never-ending pressure to reciprocate. You might feel uncomfortable when you receive more than you give. And if you don't receive something in return, you may feel exploited.

There can be some drawbacks to being Selfless. Sometimes it will create risk and place you in danger. You may find yourself emotionally overwhelmed by caring for and helping others. You may give too much, depleting your energy, reserves, and resources, and develop destructive behaviors that overwhelm you. While you may practice a Selfless act with good intentions, it may not lead to the helpful outcome you anticipated. And if done too often, it may lead you to focus your efforts on one cause while neglecting others, and you may neglect your own financial, physical, or social needs to care for others as well.

Despite these potential issues, Selfless behavior is a skill worth developing. As you treat others and the world like you would treat yourself, with kindness, generosity, and love, you receive the gifts of your humble strength and service many times over.

I act Selflessly out of concern for others.

I act from a place of moderation and self-care.

I practice random acts of kindness with no thought of reward.

"Selfless acts are a source of profound meaning for yourself and your life." –Ron Kaufman

"Change comes when humanity becomes Self-LESS." –Pamela J. Wells

"Selfless love is always costly, fear can't afford it, pride doesn't understand it, and friends never forget it." –Bob Goff

MEPSS Activities

Mental – It's important to accept that you may be wrong, don't have all the answers, and don't always know what is best. Bring to mind an occasion when this was true for you. What does this bring up in you? What did you learn from this experience? What can you put into practice for similar occasions in the future? Affirm your growth and learning by giving yourself a hug.

Emotional – List 10 inspirational people who regularly engage in Selfless acts. What emotions do their Selfless acts evoke in you? How do they touch you, and why? What do you admire about each person? What quality or qualities would you like to develop? How will you use this emotional power to offer a Selfless act of your own?

Physical – How can you show Selfless love* to others while still showing Selfless love* to yourself? What personal boundaries* do you need to put into place so that you can still make yourself available to your family and friends while not letting others take advantage of you? What acts of generosity and benevolence might tempt you to overstep this boundary line and move your actions from Selfless to the need to feel loved and appreciated? Journal your thoughts and observe your actions this week.

Social – You want to do something to meet a need*, which is great. What is harder is to do something that eliminates the cause of the distress or issue. What social cause tugs at your heart? What organization or group working to eliminate the cause will you offer your Selfless service to? Commit to your first action today.

Spiritual – Most spiritual traditions encourage practicing Selfless acts as part of spiritual growth and development. Explore 3 traditions. Note what a Selfless act is called in each, and the similarities, and differences between them. Then choose one to participate in. What differences did you notice in yourself? How did it touch the humanity in your heart? What one action will you take based on what you learned about yourself?

Selfless

Self-Wounding

Self-Wounding is recognizing the pain you drag around like a ball and chain that provokes the healing possibility to free and transform into the gift of promised love.

Self-Wounding is a blessing that comes in the form of a wound. The wound is probably not your fault, but its healing is your responsibility. It is a deep part of your essence that prompts and perhaps forces you to take the first step, recognizing that there is indeed a wound, and then to take a second step and do something about it. Once faced, embraced, and cared for (dare I say loved and accepted for what it offers), it creates the motivational force toward ongoing growth and transformation as the Simply Self-Wonderful YOU!

Self-Wounding blocks you and ends up wounding you in the process. Wounding is part of life and comes in many forms, many more than the ones focused on here. Sometimes these Self-Woundings are the most important parts of life, as they offer so many gifts by which to grow, mature, stretch, and reflect on who you are and who you want to become. They often become reasons why people say they wouldn't have done anything differently when they reflect on their lives. Yet, you may want to do something differently now and acknowledge your wounds and begin to heal them through compassion, love, and healing work.

Self-Wounding and healing are not opposites; they are part of the same process. Your wounds enable you to be compassionate toward the wounds of others. Your limitations make you aware of the limitations of others. Your Self-Woundings are lessons to learn and grow from, not be ashamed or embarrassed by or to fight against. They are there to accept and love, for they are the imperfections that make up the perfectly imperfect beloved human and Divine child you are.

For when you show someone your heart, your past, your wounds, and they show you theirs, you have entrusted each other with the honor of sharing the deepest part of yourselves. This allows you to release the pain you drag around like a ball and chain and provokes the healing possibility to free and transform every wounding, big and small, into the gift of promised love.

I am a perfectly imperfect beloved child of God.

I transform my wounds into gifts for growth and transformation.

I offer compassion and love to my wounded places.

"A broken heart heals when we allow the healing to go as deep as the wound went." –Beth Moore

"Turn your wounds into wisdom." –Oprah Winfrey

"When someone shows you their heart, their past, their wounds, they have entrusted you with the deepest part of themselves. It is the part of themselves that makes them uniquely beautiful. To be trusted in this way is a great honor. Guard that trust with your life." – Yasmin Mogamed

MEPSS Activities

Mental – How have your deepest wounds transformed you into someone you are not? What are the rationalizations you have told yourself? Now write a counter to each of those rationalizations that will enable you to transform yourself into who you truly are.

Emotional – Make a list of the Self-Woundings that remain unacknowledged and unwept over. Choose one to acknowledge. Create a 'badge of honor' with a special design that has meaning for you. Be creative. Place it in a place where you can honor it daily. When the time is right, honor it by weeping for it in a safe, protected space. You may want to collect your tears and honor them too.

Physical – Take a wound inventory. Scan your body for any scars. What story do those scars tell you? Now consider all the wounds you have received that never show on your body but are deeper and more hurtful. What story are you carrying around for each of those? Choose two and shift the story to one of healing and liberation.

Social – You may have rattled off the adage, 'Sticks and stones may break my bones, but words will never hurt me.' What phrases, names, and other harmful words have you been called? How did those make you feel? What was the impact of those words on your life? Now reverse the questions. What phrases, names, and other harmful words have you said to others? How did this make you feel? How do you think it made the other person feel? Write an apology to yourself and the other person. If you decide to apologize, consider beforehand if it will cause further wounding or if it can help you heal.

Spiritual – Use your favorite Healing Light meditation or find one to listen to online to access and engage the powerful healing network within you. If you can, listen to it at least twice a day, once in the morning and once in the evening, for a week or until you feel healed and free.

Self-Absorption

Self-Absorption is the Self-Wounding that shrinks your world so tightly that you miss out on the expansive gift of others and the larger world.

If you have been called self-absorbed, it is usually not meant as a compliment but is a way of saying you are self-preoccupied, Self-Centered, self-obsessed, and even egotistical and Selfish. It labels you as someone preoccupied with yourself and your own life who doesn't show much concern about anyone or anything outside your narrow self-interest. You don't make much effort to listen or understand other people's thoughts and feelings, and you don't make the best of friends.

However, Self-Absorption is better understood as a way you try to protect yourself from feeling insecure, threatened, and vulnerable, which causes you to doubt yourself and feel inadequate. Overly analytical thoughts about yourself and feelings of fear about being powerless, unworthy, flawed, or out of control produce anxiety, shame, and a general sense of helplessness which you try to protect yourself from by focusing solely on yourself.

Because of the fear, you try to hide how you are and show others only the best and most captivating part of your personality. You think you are great and don't want anyone to see the hidden elements that make you secretly insecure. You focus on all the wrongs the world has done to you and never accept responsibility for your part in it.

As a result of your Self-Absorption, you have trouble with intimacy and a hard time understanding the thoughts, feelings, needs, and desires of others and have difficulty appreciating the world that exists outside of your small inward-directed focus. When you spend all your time focusing on your own personal contentment and happiness to the exclusion of others, all of this anxiety, stress, and obsession will lead to depression, health problems, and earlier death.

A more neutral way of looking at Self-Absorption can be therapeutic and even necessary as you pay attention to your wants and needs appropriately. It can become a healthy practice of Self-Reflection, Self-Awareness, and introspection of your personality characteristics to gain valuable personal insight and growth into maturity. When Self-Absorption is viewed this way, it becomes a gift of truly knowing and accepting yourself that offers inner peace. When you stand in Self-Absorption this way, you can now see the bigger picture, the expansive gift of others, appreciate nurturing intimate relationships, and join with others to work for growth, resilience, and the transformation of the larger world.

I take time each day to look around me.

I notice the good things others are doing in the world.

I take care of myself in a balanced and healthy way.

"Serving others breaks you free from the shackles of self and self-absorption that choke out the joy of living." –John Hope Bryant

"Shatter the glass. In our society that is so self-absorbed, begin to look less at yourself and more at each other. Learn more about the face of your neighbor and less about your own." –Sargent Shriver

"Loving yourself...does not mean being self-absorbed or narcissistic, or disregarding others. Rather it means welcoming yourself as the most honored guest in your own heart, a guest worthy of respect, a lovable companion." –Margot Anand

MEPSS Activities

Mental – Is your Saboteur* berating you for past mistakes and shortcomings? Are you comparing yourself to others in a way that makes you superior? Are you worried about what the future holds? Choose one of these thought streams and talk back to it in a conversation by writing with both your dominant and non-dominant hand*. Your dominant hand will be the thoughts you are having. Your non-dominant hand will be the voice of your loving Higher Power or Sacred Voice of the Divine*.

Emotional – If you have been feeling depressed or anxious and you have found yourself acting rude or inconsiderate to others, understand that something is going on deep underneath these feelings and symptoms. What needs are not being met? How can you meet this need in a healthy way? This may also be a good time to speak to a mental health professional* who can explore deeper with you.

Physical – Move your body! Dance, mime, swim, climb a tree or play on playground equipment. Be fascinated with how your body works – each part individually and in cooperation with other parts. Enjoy the physical movement and the freedom you feel from letting your thoughts and emotions go for just this little while.

Social – Instead of turning the conversation back on yourself, even when it's not about you, remember to take a moment to pause. Return to the present moment; feel yourself in your body, not your head. Focus on what the other person is sharing and really listen. Nod, keep eye contact, and offer kind words of support and encouragement. Afterward, compliment yourself and name 3 things you found fascinating about the other person in the conversation.

Spiritual – Try to notice the wonder around you for the next week or so. Listen to music and lose yourself in the notes, melody line, or beat. Visit a museum and stand in front of a piece of artwork or sculpture. Look at it from all sides, up close and farther away. Contemplate what the artist might have been thinking or what this piece is saying to you.

SELF-ABSORPTION

Self-Abuse

Self-Abuse is the Self-Wounding war going on inside your head that denies the white flag of surrender that wins back the gift of your worth and status as a beloved human being.

Self-Abuse includes any behavior that causes you damage or harm to yourself. It may be intentional and physical such as directly injuring your body, or more indirect and even unintentional, using words and thoughts to devalue and compromise your mental or emotional health.

Entertaining negativity about your circumstances, yourself, and your relationships is the most common form of Self-Abuse. Constantly telling yourself you are ugly and unworthy or staying with a partner that berates or demeans you are examples of mental and emotional Self-Abuse. Self-Abuse is rampant in our culture. It is slightly higher in females but is followed closely by males. Self-Abuse is an attempt to cope with a problem but does not address the problem itself.

You abuse your imagination when you imagine yourself as less than you are. You begin to create a Self-Image that is so much less than who you really are, and then you begin to believe it and act from it. You deny your full potential when you make statements like 'I can't do that,' I'll never be able to,' or 'I don't deserve this' (deserving is always a judgment statement). Another creation of your imagination is something you fear – the worst-case scenario and all the 'what ifs' that are just scare tactics that add worry or anxiety and masquerade as careful and detailed 'planning' or being careful. You use your imagination against yourself by creating Self-Images that deny the best or most brilliant dream for your future self.

The good news is that you can break this emotionally abusive cycle. It begins with admitting that you no longer want to mentally and emotionally treat yourself this way. You acknowledge how powerful you are by choosing to honor, love, and respect yourself. And by choosing to eliminate people and situations that are not for your highest good, you take further control and responsibility for your own life and health and celebrate the Self-Wonderful of Self-Worth, Self-Acceptance, Self-Appreciation, Self-Care, and so many more! Congratulations, you win back the gift of your worth and status as a beloved human being.

My feelings are real and important and must be listened to.

There are good reasons for my pain, and I can get the support I need to deal with it.

I am a real, worthwhile, and good person with the right to be respected and cared for.

"Self-abuse is an infringement on one's own destiny caused by either ignorance about oneself or negligence of one's purpose!" –Israelmore Ayivor

"You have so much pain inside yourself that you try and hurt yourself on the outside because you want help." –Princess Diana

"Rehashing thoughts of painful events from the past or imagining negative events of the future is self-abuse and can be more destructive than physical harm." –Maddy Malhotra

MEPSS Activities

Mental – When thinking about yourself too much, read the story of someone you admire. If you can, read it out loud, using an expressive voice and tone to drown out the critical voice in your head.

Emotional – Draw the way you are feeling. Then, go deeper and ask your drawing what you get from emotionally abusing yourself. Next, draw that answer and ask that drawing, "What is a better way to get what I truly need?" You can also draw that or take the first step in meeting that need.

Physical – Try this progressive muscle relaxation exercise. Sit or lie down and make yourself comfortable. Begin with your toes and clench them for a count of 5, then relax them for a count of 5. Then offer your toes a compliment for all the work that they do for you. Then move up to your calves, thighs, hips, and abdominal area. Then make fists with your fingers for 5 counts, then relax them for a count of 5, tense your arm muscles, complimenting yourself on your strength, then relax them. Move up to your face and have fun making faces by tightening your facial muscles. When you relax them, make sighing or other noises that offer a sense of release. Don't forget to include your neck, moving it from side to side, lowering your chin, then lifting it up. Notice how you feel now.

Social – Cut emotionally abusive people from your life by practicing this simple figure 8 technique for establishing boundaries*. You can either draw a figure 8 (or an infinity symbol) on a piece of paper or just trace it with your finger in your other hand. Visualize yourself in the center of one of the circles surrounded by golden light. In the center of the other circle, place the person, strong emotion, negative self-talk, or traumatic memory and surround it with golden light. Now visualize a blue neon light that moves around the circles of golden light, following the direction of the figure 8. The golden and blue neon light help to contain and set boundaries around your energy and begin to separate you from the other's energy. Do this for several minutes, 2-3 times daily for several weeks. Doing it when you wake up and when you go to bed allows the subconscious mind to do the deep work of separation. When you feel ready, and only when you do (this may take months or years), imagine scissors cutting the ties that bind you and sense yourself standing alone in the fullness of yourself.

Spiritual – Find a guided meditation on YouTube or another audible platform and let it calm and nurture you in the moment. As you feel calm, relaxed, and more in touch with yourself, reach out for support from a mental health professional*, therapist*, counselor, coach, group, or person you trust you can talk to. Call the crisis prevention line and get immediate help if you are in crisis.

SELF-
ABUSE

Self-Centered

Self-Centered is the Self-Wounding of using a microscope on yourself that becomes a gift of discovering the genuine you when staying grounded and centered in your life.

Self-Centered can go both ways. It can be both a Self-Wounding and a Self-Wonderful. As a Self-Centered person, you can be excessively concerned with yourself and your own needs. You can completely ignore the needs of others and only do what is best for yourself. This kind of Self-Centeredness is often driven by a primal pain that says you are not worthy or safely connected to others.

This kind of Self-Centeredness is costly. It is at the root of many mental health issues and addictions. It damages relationships because you cannot be empathic or caring about another person, only yourself. It becomes a vicious cycle when your excessive concerns about yourself cause more anxiety, which keeps your capacity to tune in and pay attention to others at a low to non-existent level. It leads to disconnection and continues the downward spiral into further Self-Centered thoughts and behaviors.

Being Self-Centered is very present in our culture, which emphasizes individualism. And yet, remember that you would not be alive without assistance and support from others. When you act from this type of Self-Centered behavior, you take little or no time to understand another person's point of view or feeling. You put your own happiness first. You may even go so far as to lie or manipulate to get your way or make things work out in a way that favors you. You are trying to provide Self-Worth, Self-Love and other Self-Wonderfuls from an external source rather than the internal one of you.

There is another way of being a Self-Centered person that can serve you well. It is an internal source that is life-centered. In this way, you are the constant in your own life. In this life-centered, grounded way of being Self-Centered, you discover the genuine you and have the potential to be even more generous and make even greater contributions to the people and world around you.

I am centered in myself, making the best choice for me right now.

I stay centered in myself, no matter the circumstances.

My Self-Centeredness creates harmony with everyone around me.

"Too much self-centered attitude brings isolation. It results in loneliness, fear, anger. The extreme self-centered attitude is the source of suffering." –Dalai Lama

"The change from self-centeredness to human-centeredness is the key to peaceful existence." –Lailah Gifty Akita

"The selfish and self-centered have a hard time being kind, even though you and I know that kindness is a source of relief to the soul." –Janvier Couteu-Chando

MEPSS Activities

Mental – What do you think about all day? If it's mostly about you, you may suffer from excessive Self-Centeredness. Do not beat yourself up about it; otherwise, you will give yourself yet another reason to be self-preoccupied. Instead, practice mindfulness. Become mindful of your underlying pain. Then feel compassion for your pain. Do not take it personally. You are the product of a very Self-Centered culture! This will defuse any associated shame and unhook you from this type of Self-Centered thought pattern. Now you are free to cultivate Self-Love and all those other Self-Wonderfuls that keep you Self-Centered in a life-centered affirming way.

Emotional – Healing an excessive tendency to be Self-Centered begins with an intentional daily practice of Self-Love. Devote yourself to loving yourself fully, completely, and unconditionally by cultivating the feeling of love* that arises with the practice of stillness. Stand in your life-centered, Self-Centered place and simply sense and notice what arises when you infuse your consciousness with this kind of love. Do it over and over again. You will begin to experience a gradual transformation from feeling excessively Self-Centered to that supportive life-centered Self-Centered that you can now confidently stand in.

Physical – Go ahead! Make yourself the center of attention. Be as Self-Centered as you want! Look at yourself in the mirror. Stand on a stage. Make a video. Make all the funny faces, physical gestures, and non-verbal expressions you use when you want people to pay attention to you. Notice how you feel when you offer these back to yourself. What needs were met by your excessive Self-Centered actions? What needs were not met? Now ask yourself, 'How have I tried and failed to meet this need with excessive Self-Centered behavior? What would be a better (and even perhaps fun) way to meet this need?

Social – Often, instead of being centered in ourselves, we are 'other-centered;' spouse-centered, children-centered, work-centered, service-centered, or even past-centered or future-centered. When you are, you are taking on other people's energy* and not being 100% full of yourself. Who are you thinking about right now? Do the practice of Neutral Separations* with them and center yourself in the present moment and independent of any outside force or influence. Center yourself in your life-centered, Self-Centered space of now.

Spiritual – Find a nearby labyrinth and make a date with yourself to walk it. Walk toward the center and stay in the center for as long as you desire, sensing yourself at the center of your life, the center of your world, the center of the universe. If you wish, ask the Divine presence of the universe* to stand with you, to give you the strength, power, and love to stay permanently Self-Centered in your life. Try to walk the labyrinth with others to experience being Self-Centered with others in their own Self-Centered space, walking but not merging with you. As you walk back out, allow the power and insights of the experience to sink fully into your heart and life-centered, Self-Centered consciousness.

Self-Condemnation

Self-Condemnation is the Self-Wounding that happens when you throw yourself out with the garbage that denies celebrating you as the gift of the priceless treasure found at a yard sale.

Self-Condemnation is blaming yourself for something you failed to do or something you know you should do. It is also blaming yourself for not being the person you 'shoulda, coulda, woulda' been in the situation. There is a lot of 'shoulding' and shame in Self-Condemnation.

Self-Condemnation keeps you inward-focused and constantly analyzing what you could have done differently. It magnifies your shortcomings and perceived failures. You are overly serious about making mistakes. You disgrace and dishonor yourself and want to hide from everyone. You become immobilized by fear and disempowered by guilt and shame. You become weary, angry, and resentful. Your best self has left the building long ago, and you feel like trash to throw into the garbage. You are attacking yourself as if you were found to be utterly unacceptable by society and despicable as a person. This is never the truth and is once again the voice of your Saboteur, your inner critic, and the weight of never being able to feel acceptable to yourself.

The work of this Self-Wounding is to use curiosity, confidence, and creativity to open your mind and heart to understanding for learning, healing, and living a happier and more fulfilling life. It is releasing the condemnation, disappointment, frustration, and self-sabotage and shifting your beliefs to succeed and act properly, reliably, and trustworthy. You no longer waste your time and energy in the 'shoulda, coulda, woulda' land of failure and regret. You take personal responsibility for all you are and have a sense of true humility. You begin to open into a broader field of awareness and feel more hopeful and energized. You begin to trust yourself more and become more resolute in who you are and your capabilities. This begins the transformation into the gifts of the Self-Wonderfuls: Self-Acceptance, Self-Appreciation, Self-Compassion, Self-Confidence, Self-Love, Self-Respect, and Self-Understanding as you become the priceless treasure you truly are.

I am a perfectly imperfect, beloved human being, and that is enough.

I release the past and step into the future with love, compassion, and kindness.

I can heal from the hurt and pain of what I have caused.

"Labels start out as little threads of self-dissatisfaction but ultimately weave together into a straightjacket of self-condemnation." –Lysa TerKeurst

"The secret of pleasure in life, as distinct from its great triumphs of transcendent joy, is to live in a series of small, legitimate successes. By legitimate I mean such as are not accompanied by self-condemnation." –Sydney Thompson Dobell

"Love yourself! The idea of becoming somebody else is based in self-hatred, in self condemnation." –Osho Shree Rajneesh

MEPSS Activities

Mental – Learn to recognize when you are condemning yourself. Notice the thoughts you believe to be true, which are distorted or lies. Recognize that your beliefs do not equal truths. Write down 5 thoughts you have believed to be true. Then write down 5 statements that counter those misbeliefs and lies. Practice telling yourself the new statement and erase the old misbeliefs by writing them on paper and tearing them up, cutting them into tiny pieces, burning them, or immersing them in water until the paper falls apart.

Emotional – Explore the question – Whose standards are you using to determine whether or not you are acceptable? Then explore what would be 'good enough' for you. Create a symbol or find a picture that represents 'good enough' and make it your cell phone wallpaper.

Physical – What activities encourage your Self-Condemnation? What specific person, thought, or action prompts your Self-Condemning thoughts and behavior? How can you do them differently? What do you need to put in place so you do not do them?

Social – What people and places tend to prompt the thoughts and feelings that lead you to Self-Condemnation? Was there a specific instance you carry with you that makes you feel unredeemable? Make amends by talking with them and asking for forgiveness*. And if you cannot make amends to the person or people you harmed, do something good for someone else. And by all means, take the first step in self-forgiveness*.

Spiritual – Explore the Divine/God/Higher Power/Mystery/Spirit/Source/Universe*. What kind of God did you experience growing up? What is your concept now? What kind of God would you like to believe in? Find a spiritual or religious center that believes and teaches that people are flawed but inherently good, not only lovable but also inherently loved. Have a conversation with one of the leaders about learning more about this kind of Divine presence and a practice or two that can foster feelings of lovingkindness to yourself.

Self-Condemnation

Self-Criticism

Self-Criticism is the Self-Wounding that looks at every crack and flaw that hides the gift, value, and quality of the beautifully cut diamond you were created to be.

Self-Criticism is the behavior you have developed over your lifetime of pointing out your perceived flaws. This can be in many areas such as physical appearance, behavior, intellectual capabilities, personality, ability to handle relationships, school or work performance, or a myriad of other things you use to compare yourself to an imagined seemingly perfect 'other' or standard. When you criticize yourself, you threaten the core of your self-identity, who you think you are, and who you aspire to be.

Everyone has that Saboteur inner critical voice in their head. It is the inner voice of shame that has become part of your internal self-talk. Your Saboteur blames you for things that go wrong, compares you to others' achievements, abilities, and looks, and finds you less than. Your Saboteur sets impossible standards of perfection and punishes you for the smallest mistake.

The Saboteur's main purpose is to try to keep you safe. It wants you to feel in control but reinforces the illusion of control instead. It also tries to motivate you to a desired behavior but uses an attacking voice instead of an encouraging one. Your Saboteur thinks that if it is strict and puts pressure on you that you will be motivated to be and do better. But it only keeps you stuck, going in circles in your mind. It doesn't help you feel better about yourself or show you ways to grow, but it only gets increasingly worse.

Self-Criticism leads to increased procrastination and keeps you from reaching your goals. When you feel worthless and incompetent, there is little likelihood of putting in a better effort next time. You can set yourself free by understanding the underlying source of Self-Criticism and taking back your power! You can replace the inner critical voice of the Saboteur with a realistic, affirming self-statement.

While it is impossible to completely get rid of your inner critical Saboteur voice, you can learn to take away much of its power by understanding the hidden motivation behind the Self-Criticism through practicing many of the Self-Wonderfuls such as Self-Acceptance, Self-Compassion, Self-Esteem, Self-Love, Self-Regard, Self-Respect Self-Worth, and more. When you do this, you increase the value, quality, and shine of the beautiful diamond you are.

I see criticism as information that empowers me.

I choose to respond to criticism in a constructive way.

I look for the hidden motivation beneath self-criticism.

"If babies held the same tendency toward self-criticism as adults, they might never learn to walk or talk. Can you imagine infants stomping, 'Aarggh! Screwed up again!' Fortunately, babies are free of self-criticism. They just keep practicing." –Dan Millman

"Remember, you have been criticizing yourself for years, and it hasn't worked. Try approving of yourself and see what happens." –Louise L Hay

"I know quite certainly that I myself have no special talent; curiosity, obsession and dogged endurance, combined with self-criticism have brought me to my ideas." –Albert Einstein

MEPSS Activities

Mental – Become aware of any Self-Critical thoughts you are having. Just notice it for a moment or two. Notice where the thought takes you and where it goes after that. Next time that thought comes, see if you can stop it earlier and earlier with a gentle thank you that lets the thought know that you can do the same thing in a more affirming way.

Emotional – When a Self-Critical thought triggers an emotional response in your mind, respond to the Saboteur* with kindness with words as a back-and-forth dialogue (sometimes it's more clear when you write it out using the 'non-dominant hand' writing* format). Also, find an action that can reinforce your kindness to yourself. Be grateful for the help the Saboteur* has given you in the past and remind it that you are now an adult and can choose to do it in a new, more nurturing way.

Physical – Gently touch your skin somewhere on your body that feels comfortable. Then say something reassuring to yourself. The physical touch releases oxytocin that begins an automatic calming response in your body. Do this for as long as feels comfortable, then give yourself a hug and go on with your day.

Social – Ask yourself how a friend would respond when you are struggling with this problem. Then use your phone to send a voice message to yourself, offering yourself those kind, supportive, and wise words. Save it so that you can replay it whenever you want to or need support.

Spiritual – Write yourself a love letter. If you can only think of one or two things to write, that's okay: it's a start toward more later. If you want, you can write them on Post-it notes and put them in places only you will see them. Perhaps some will surprise you when you find them later!

Self-criticism

Self-Deception

Self-Deception is the Self-Wounding of a Magician's trick that convinces you with lies and false evidence, distorting the gifts of truth, honesty, and acceptance of who you are.

Self-Deception at its most basic level is lying to yourself. It may come in the form of believing things that are not true or its opposite, believing things to be true when they are not. At its core, Self-Deception is the inability to be completely honest with yourself. And the repercussions of this mean that if you are living a lie then you can't tell other people the truth of who you are.

Of course, what makes Self-Deception complicated is that it often serves a really important function. As a child you played around with the truth in your imagination or 'pretend' play—and maybe you still do! This helps you try out new personas and situations in the cause of exploration and learning more about yourself. But if you are dishonest with yourself, you will make choices based on insecurity, and the more you do that, the more you will regret your choices. You want to act from a place of security, comfort, and honesty, and when you are not strong enough to be your true self, you give up your power. You lose your ability to make choices that will lead you to who you want to be and the life you want to live.

When you act with Self-Deception, you deflect anything you don't like about yourself and project it onto other people as a way to protect yourself. Another way this manifests is through regression, meaning you go to an earlier insecure stage of emotional development to defend yourself, which is a lie because you are already capable of much more. Another is preferring to live in a dream world, seeing the world in a naïve way rather than reality. This is a form of escapism that obscures the truth and the harsh realities of real life.

Becoming aware of how you use Self-Deception is key to giving up the Magician's trick and discovering more fully who you are in your truest form, being honest, and accepting yourself as uniquely you!

I will be honest with myself and accept things as they are.

I take back my power and tell the truth.

I refuse to tell lies.

'Nothing is easier than self-deception.' –Demosthenes

"Human beings have a demonstrated talent for self-deception when their emotions are stirred." –Carl Sagan

"Suppose we were able to share meanings freely without a compulsive urge to impose our view or conform to those of others and without distortion and self-deception. Would this not constitute a real revolution in culture." –David Bohm

MEPSS Activities

Mental – When your Saboteur* voice or inner critic is speaking loudly to you, rationalizing the lies it tells, instead of trying to talk back to it, play the 'Pinocchio' game. Imagine the face of your Saboteur, and for each lie, it says add an inch to its nose. How long does its nose get in 10 seconds, 30 seconds, 1 minute? Please do not go for more than 2 minutes! Then counter those lies with their truth, imagining the nose growing smaller until it is the right size. You can also draw the nose and write the lies on paper, then tear it up as you speak the truth and banish the lies.

Emotional – What decisions have you made from an emotional place that further perpetuated some self-deception that ended badly yet is still unresolved? What emotional response led to the deception, and what was the lie underneath it? Now, from a more rational and informed place, what decision would you make if you could do it all over again? Remember these to use for a similar situation next time.

Physical – Play the 'if only' game. Name 10 things related to your body that you used self-deception by telling yourself 'if only' to get away from eating better, sleeping better, exercising, or taking care of your body. Now counter those 'if only's' with statements that will make you feel better and motivated to take better care of yourself.

Social – What are the most common ways you 'shapeshift' or deceive others when you are trying hard to fit in and be accepted in a group situation? What pattern do you see? Who do you want to show yourself to be in a group situation? Now list at least 10 true things you would like to be and show next time you're in a group and choose two to practice being and doing for next time.

Spiritual – Have some fun with the benefits of Self-Deception by imagining yourself as a child, trying on different characters in your favorite stories, fables, or fantasy realms. Use as many props or costumes as you wish to make it as real as possible. What is it like to be that character? What about that character would you like to bring into your real life? In what 3 ways will you incorporate these qualities into your life? How will you do it?

Self-
Deception

Self-Defeat

Self-Defeat is the Self-Wounding obstacle course purposely placed in your way to trip you up, move you farther away from your goals, and cause you to miss out on the gift of a fulfilling and vibrant life.

Self-Defeat is any action or behavior that sabotages your goal and is counterproductive to your best life. It can be false truths, thoughts, behaviors, and actions that you place in your way as obstacles to placate a fear of success and being fully responsible for your life.

Self-Defeat is most seen in behaviors where you try to protect yourself from perceived danger by choosing to suffer, fail at something, handicap yourself, plead helplessly, procrastinate, or fear success. Self-Defeat also happens when you neglect yourself, criticize yourself, aim for perfection, refuse help, feel self-pity, compare yourself to others or withdraw socially or alienate yourself. Self-Defeat happens through actions when you overspend, underspend, overeat, undereat, abuse alcohol or drugs, injure yourself, or engage in risky sexual behaviors. Continuing to use Self-Defeating behaviors not only moves you away from your goals but is distracting, self-sabotaging, and causes you to feel exhausted and bad about yourself. They lead to inevitable consequences, can contribute to, or even cause illness and disease, and affect your ability to be happy and fulfilled. And yet you continue to be a victim of Self-Defeat, unaware of the real need underneath.

You are not alone. The average person evokes Self-Defeat through 6 self-defeating behaviors on an ongoing basis! And most people are unaware that they are even doing them. You probably began to practice them in stressful or traumatic situations as a young child to protect yourself. You did the best you could, and they may have helped back then when you had little control and weak coping skills. Now you can learn a better way by becoming aware of what they are when you do them and why you do them. By observing and understanding why you practiced Self-Defeat, you can now welcome new ways of supporting and standing up for yourself.

Self-Defeat can be countered with life-promoting and life-giving alternatives. You begin to play a conscious choice game of replacing a self-defeating behavior with a self-enhancing one by removing the obstacles you purposely placed in your way. Then you can embrace your character strengths and grow into the best version of yourself! And in doing so, your goal of the fulfilling and amazing life you have yearned for will be the gift you can now receive in healthy and life-affirming ways.

I value myself and treat myself with respect.

I let go of all Self-Defeating thoughts.

I choose healthy instead of unhealthy ways of thinking, feeling, and acting.

"The wrong kind of praise creates a self-defeating behavior. The right kind motivates students to learn." –Carol S. Dweck

Dreaming is one thing, and working towards the dream is one thing, but working with expectations in mind is very self-defeating. –Michael Landon

I witnessed first-hand the self-defeating results of putting yourself under so much pressure to perform. –Ananya Birla

MEPSS Activities

Mental – The first step is awareness of the thoughts causing your Self-Defeating behaviors. Begin to practice mindfulness* by focusing on the present moment. As you go about your day, use Post-it notes or record your voice on your phone to list your Self-Defeating behaviors in action. If you can, add what thought triggered the Self-Defeating behavior. And then, if you can, add what happened because of it. Try to see this as just information gathering without judgment, criticism, or practicing further Self-Defeating behaviors. In other words, 'just the facts.' You want to get at your truth, not your worst fears about yourself or the world.

Emotional – Become a sleuth and go underneath the Self-Defeating behavior; imagine you are cuddling yourself as a sad, hurting young child and ask the child: 'What fear are you trying to push away, ignore, or compensate for? What do you need?' Be gentle with yourself as the child's loving mother. Go slowly; only explore one at a time. Otherwise, you will be overwhelmed and defeat the purpose of discovery and new insights.

Physical – Make a habit of appreciating and complimenting yourself by keeping your mouth shut about your so-called 'flaws.' Create a simple, easy, no-cost practice that you can do daily to show love to yourself. Then do it every day for a month until it becomes a new habit.

Social – Social media often leads to Self-Defeating thoughts. So, unplug and give yourself a break from this constant barrage. Start at five minutes and work up to an hour then to a whole weekend!

Spiritual – All Self-Defeating behaviors stem from not feeling loved. Trying to love* yourself alone is nearly impossible, as we all need someone to mirror this highest quality to us lovingly and compassionately. Reach out to a safe, supportive, and kind person who understands these behaviors to support and guide you as you work to create new healthier behaviors and patterns.

SELF-DEFEATING

Self-Denial

Self-Denial is the habitual Self-Wounding of saying 'No,' pushing away the gifts that are meant for your enjoyment, fulfillment, and flourishing in life.

Self-Denial is a pattern of Self-Sabotage you choose regularly to keep yourself from experiencing the joy and fulfillment you are truly meant to have. It is a willingness to forgo doing or having something that would offer you pleasure. It becomes a form of being morally good through self-sacrifice when you believe that by refusing to do or have something participating, you have increased the good for another person.

In its simplest form, Self-Denial is not admitting to an issue of concern. When you deny a problem exists, then you don't have to feel bad about the fact that there is a problem. This is a defense mechanism that discharges anxiety and emotional discomfort. But it doesn't solve anything or make your life better. So, it's important to look at and name the need or needs underneath the Self-Denial that is not being met.

The issues can be about being in control, numbing pain, needing love or acceptance, not feeling good enough, not valuing yourself, protection, or something missing in life. Self-Denial is often related to a past experience that now shows up in a pattern of behavior. This includes staying in an abusive relationship, addiction, eating disorders, financial issues, obesity, sex, and shopping. One pattern is blaming another person and seeing yourself as a victim. Another is attacking and invalidating a person, so you don't have to acknowledge they have made a good point or suggestion. A third one is living in the past and not seeing what will eventually be needed to be accepted. Another is being unable to forgive oneself or another to mend or release a relationship.

The good news is that Self-Denial can be transformed from a Self-Wounding by offering yourself gifts that put you in charge of your thoughts and feelings. It gives you the power and choice to change them. It means finding other healthier ways to receive what the Self-Denial was giving you in an unhealthy way. You can find guidance by creating values and ideas that better align with who you want to become by reflecting on the energy of your desire, saying 'Yes' to using the gifts of the Self-Wonderfuls that are meant for your true enjoyment, fulfillment, and flourishing in life.

I choose to create the life I truly desire.

I give myself what I need to truly thrive.

I can choose what offers me joy, peace, and contentment in life.

"One is happy as a result of one's own efforts, once one knows of the necessary ingredients of happiness-simple tastes, a certain degree of courage, self-denial to a point, love of work, and, above all, a clear conscience. Happiness is no vague dream; of that I now feel certain." –George Sand

"Female health issues stem from 'denial of the self and rejecting femininity.'" –Doreen Virtue

"Self-denial is painful for a moment but very agreeable in the end." –Jane Taylor

MEPSS Activities

Mental – What does healthy Self-Denial look like for you? What does unhealthy Self-Denial look like for you? What is the determining 'cross-over' point from healthy to unhealthy? At what point does it become unhealthy for you? What is the line you cross? When do you most often fall into unhealthy Self-Denial? Be aware when you begin to do this next time.

Emotional – Look at one of your close relationships and ask yourself, 'When do I deny too much of myself for the sake of the other person's happiness, but not my own?' What emotions and feelings do you experience when you deny too much of yourself? Choose 5 new, more affirming responses and notice the benefits of happiness, health, and success that follow.

Physical – What areas of your body have given you concern or trouble in the past? How do these areas connect with unhealthy thoughts you or others have told you? Choose one area to focus on and do an online search for *Heal Your Body* by Louise Hay*, an early pioneer in connecting problems of the body to mental causes and new thought patterns to practice. Then practice this affirmation regularly and note the results.

Social – Blaming others, seeing yourself as the victim, and not taking responsibility for your actions is a common form of self-denial. List 10 people, organizations, or systems you most often blame rather than take responsibility for yourself. Own up to your part, apologize if necessary, and name and commit to 10 new ways to claim your part in your actions.

Spiritual – Take a few minutes to offer yourself a guided meditation. Imagine a loving, benevolent voice speaking these words to you directly and sincerely.

Your name inserted here; imagine you are fully loved, accepted, and beautiful for who you are, just as you are. Open to that sensation, welcome it in by giving this feeling of love to yourself in whatever way you want. Open and expand your heart to receive love in its fullest sense, offering appreciation, compassion, ease, forgiveness, gentleness, grace, gratitude, kindness, patience, trust, understanding, and whatever else you need. See yourself radiating love inward to all those parts of you that you have denied and been unkind to over your life. You are Simply Self-Wonderful.

Self-
Denial

Self-Deprecation

Self-Deprecation is the Self-Wounding comedy show that laughs off, devalues, and disparages the gifts of your value, talents, and accomplishments that need a better stage.

Self-Deprecation is when you repeatedly make fun of your imperfections in a playful or serious way. You laugh at things you hate about your appearance, personality, talents, and anything you can't accept about yourself.

Self-Deprecation is a way to play yourself down to peers, colleagues, and loved ones to appear humble, gain support, or protect yourself from other people's digs and criticisms before they make them. When this happens, you undermine your authority and choose others' opinions over your own. And often, staying silent about your abilities and achievements can have unwanted consequences for yourself and others that may relate to you. In the long term, the more often Self-Deprecation becomes internalized attacks on yourself, the more it can harm your health and well-being.

When the consequence of Self-Deprecation leads to feeling constantly ashamed of yourself for no good reason and apologizing for yourself constantly, you feel insecure about many parts of yourself. You may even think you are the reason for your problems and struggles and blame yourself or become angry for being unable to do better. This can lead to depression and isolation. And it impacts your physical health as well, especially your immune system. Self-Deprecation often accompanies other Self-Woundings, such as Self-Criticism, Self-Doubt, Self-Humiliation, Self-Judgment, Self-Loathing, and Self-Sabotage. It also undermines many of the Self-Wonderfuls you need, such as Self-Acceptance, Self-Appreciation, Self-Compassion, Self-Empowerment, Self-Esteem, Self-Expression, Self-Regard, Self-Respect, and Self-Worth.

The good news is that you can choose to become your own best friend by reminding yourself that you are a perfectly imperfect, loved human being that makes mistakes and that you are okay as you are. You can watch what you say about yourself and begin to shift your hurtful self-talk to more affirming and loving language. You can choose to see your so-called 'flaws' as gifts for growth and learning. You can choose another stage to stand on and show yourself as you truly are; valued, talented, and accomplished in your own unique way!

I use my humor and playfulness to love and affirm all of who I am.

My perceived imperfections make me the unique, beautiful, and beloved person I am.

I let go of self-deprecation and practice true humility.

"Self-deprecation is not an answer to keeping one's balance. I think that it's very damaging." –Viola Davis

"We live in a world of self-deprecation, and while it's healthy to make fun of ourselves from time to time, it bothers me when I see women of all ages belittling their accomplishments because they don't want to appear boastful or overconfident.... There is absolutely no shame in being proud of what you've managed to achieve. Own it!" –Lea Michele

"I think women have a hard time not apologizing their way into negotiations. We tend to back in to these conversations in a self-deprecating and ultimately self-defeating way." –Mika Brzezinski

MEPSS Activities

Mental – List 10 phrases that you use to downplay your talents and accomplishments. Now change each of them into a supportive and constructive statement.

Emotional – Self-Deprecation can relieve emotional stress by making you laugh as a coping mechanism. Notice when you tend to be Self-Deprecating and follow the moment back to the point of emotional stress. What made you do it? What were the fears or negative thoughts that prompted it? What is underneath it? Trace it to its origin, if possible, and then find a healthy way to satisfy that need.

Physical – Comedy is Self-Deprecation. Go ahead and be the comedian and have a comedy show about yourself. Make up 10 ten Self-Deprecating jokes and tell them to yourself in the mirror or by making a video with your phone. Notice how you tell them and your body language, then how you feel when you listen to the replay.

Social – Focus on the good by accepting compliments from others about you. Say, 'Thank you' – period. Accept the compliment at its face value. Record them with your phone or make a note of them. Write them down on Post-it notes and place them where you will see them and smile. See how many you can collect.

Spiritual – Every time you notice yourself being Self-Deprecating, put 50 cents in a jar. Every time you counter it with something affirming, take out 25 cents. When the jar is full, count the money, round it up to an amount that feels good to you, and donate it to a cause that helps others.

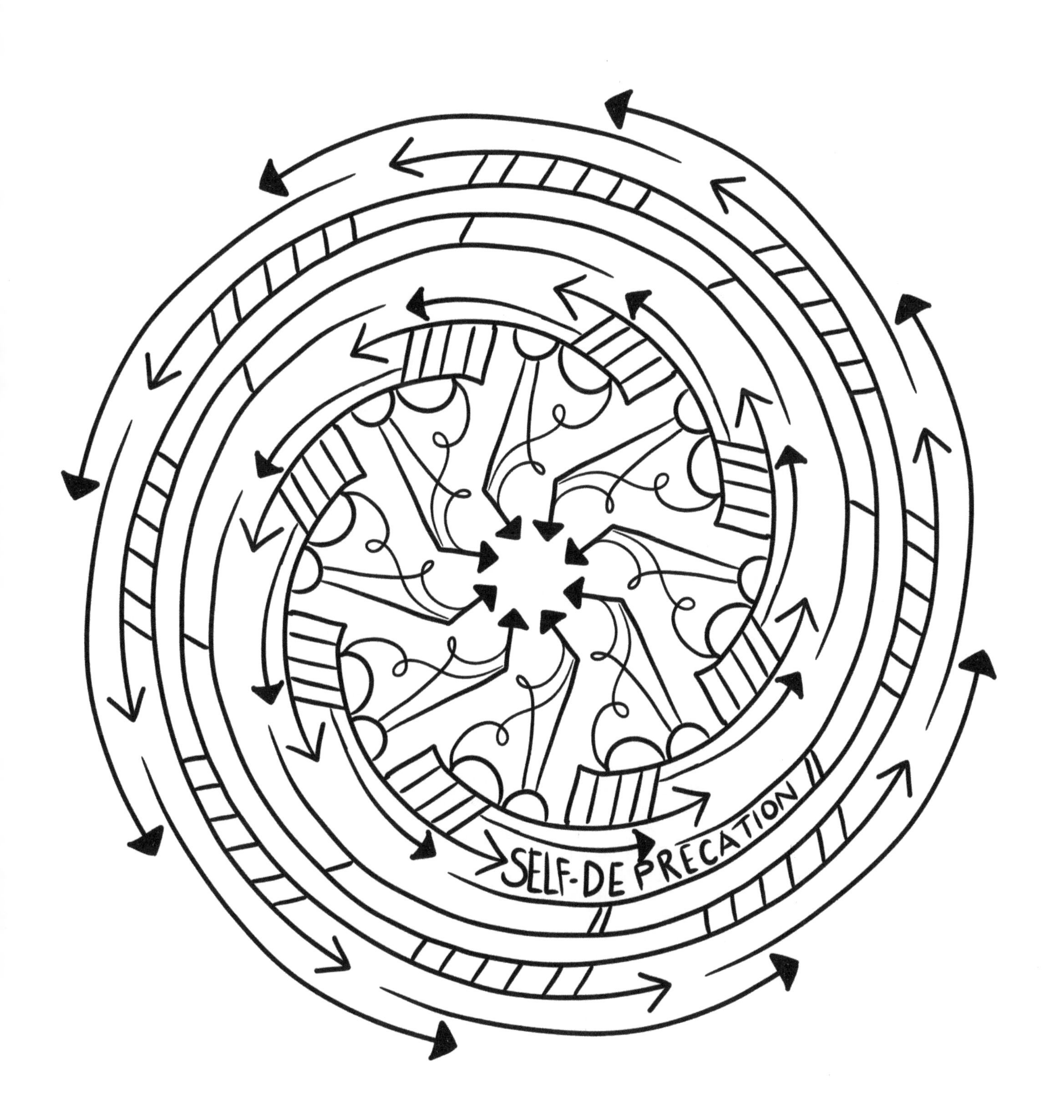
SELF-DEPRECATION

Self-Destruction

Self-Destruction is the impulsive, habitual Self-Wounding that bulldozes through your life, causing great devastation, and denying the gifts of health and happiness that help you thrive.

Self-Destruction is any behavior that is harmful to yourself. It may be deliberate, habitual, or impulsive as an attempt to turn off the emotional pain of feeling 'too much.'

You have strong urges to engage in the behavior to make the discomfort and pain stop. All you want to do is feel relief, but this only helps for a short time as the emotions keep building with increasing pressure until it becomes unbearable. And often, it doesn't make the pain disappear but worsens it. And yet, you still do the same things over and over again. Sometimes you don't even know what you are doing is causing harm until it becomes serious and damaging to your body, mind, and spirit.

Besides the common Self-Destructive behaviors of substance abuse, leading to addiction, other Self-Destructive behaviors can include: anxiety, alienating yourself from others, being late for work, clinging to an ex-partner, complaining, compulsive gambling, emotional manipulation, failing to take action, faked incompetence, jealousy, losing job after job, neediness, not taking care of the basic needs of your body, over or under eating, overspending, picking a fight, possessiveness, pushing away people you love, procrastination, refusing to exercise, refusing help, road rage, self-defeating mindsets, and other Self-Woundings, sleeping too little and poorly, social suicide, stalking, withdrawal, and violence as a way to validate your identity. The goal is to learn other ways to practice better ways to affirm your identity and who you are.

As you read this list, you may be thinking to yourself. 'There is something inherently wrong with me.' Far from it, you are human, and you've unconsciously adopted these to protect yourself against mental or emotional blame that occurred early in your childhood from family or society. It's not your fault, and you aren't to blame. And it's your choice whether to continue or to get professional help. You can start by noticing what triggers your self-destructive behaviors and choose to do something different. It can be as simple as deep breathing, hugging yourself, or listening to some music that calms you. Offering yourself compassion and forgiveness will halt the Self-Wounding bulldozer and help you feel better about yourself. Being mindful and taking one step at a time will help you make progress by decreasing the frequency, intensity, and Self-Destructive behavior. Using the Self-Wonderfuls will also support you by offering you the gifts of health and happiness to thrive, for you are Simply Self-Wonderful!

I love and honor all parts of myself.

I protect myself in new, healthy ways.

I make choices to act for my highest health and happiness.

"When we meet real tragedy in life, we can react in two ways – either by losing hope and falling into self-destructive habits, or by using the challenge to find our inner strength. Thanks to the teachings of Buddha, I have been able to take this second way." –Dalai Lama

"It's important to recognize your own self-destructive behavior and be honest about it. You're only hurting yourself or losing out on your truth and happiness. I'm not afraid to face my own personal stuff. It's so important to dig it up and figure it out and move on." –Christina Aguilera

"It's not uncool to worry about people who seem like they're going on the wrong path. There's nothing cool about being self-destructive." –Patti Smith

MEPSS Activities

Mental – List the thoughts that come when you feel fear about something. Choose the top 3. Now, list the responses that you usually take to the 3 top thoughts. If any of them are Self-Destructive responses, counter that response with a Self-Affirming thought and nurturing response.

Emotional – What part of you needs forgiveness*? Notice where the feeling is most intensely located in your body and simply accept it as it is. Now, name the hurt simply and truthfully. Don't get caught up in the story. Don't justify. Just name it. Then offer that wounded place caring, kindness, love, and forgiveness. Say to that part as part of your whole body, mind, and spirit, 'I forgive you.' 'I free you as I free myself.' 'Thank you for this lesson on how to forgive and heal myself.'

Physical – Sometimes, you overdo a good thing, and it ends up hurting you rather than helping you. What is something you overdo that results in long-term health issues if continued? Explore the motivating why underneath by asking yourself, 'Why can't I stop doing this? What is the emotion that triggers it? What is the need I'm trying to meet? How can I meet that need in a healthier, more supportive way?' You might want to consult a health care practitioner* to work with you if you get stuck.

Social – Who is someone that encourages your Self-Destructive behaviors? Write out what you might say to them or make a practice video to feel more comfortable talking with them in person. Do not do this by text, email, or any other non-physical face-to-face way. This is your life, and it is important for both of you! Explain why it's important for you to stop and why you have chosen them to join you. Then work together to find and practice new healthier behaviors. List 3 ways you will practice healthier, Self-Affirming behaviors and when you will do them each day.

Spiritual – What are you afraid to face up to? Where does the fear originate? What can you tell that small child you were as the loving, caring parent now? If you haven't experienced much love in your life, find a spiritual center that talks about love and has activities that can help you feel loved and accepted for who you are.

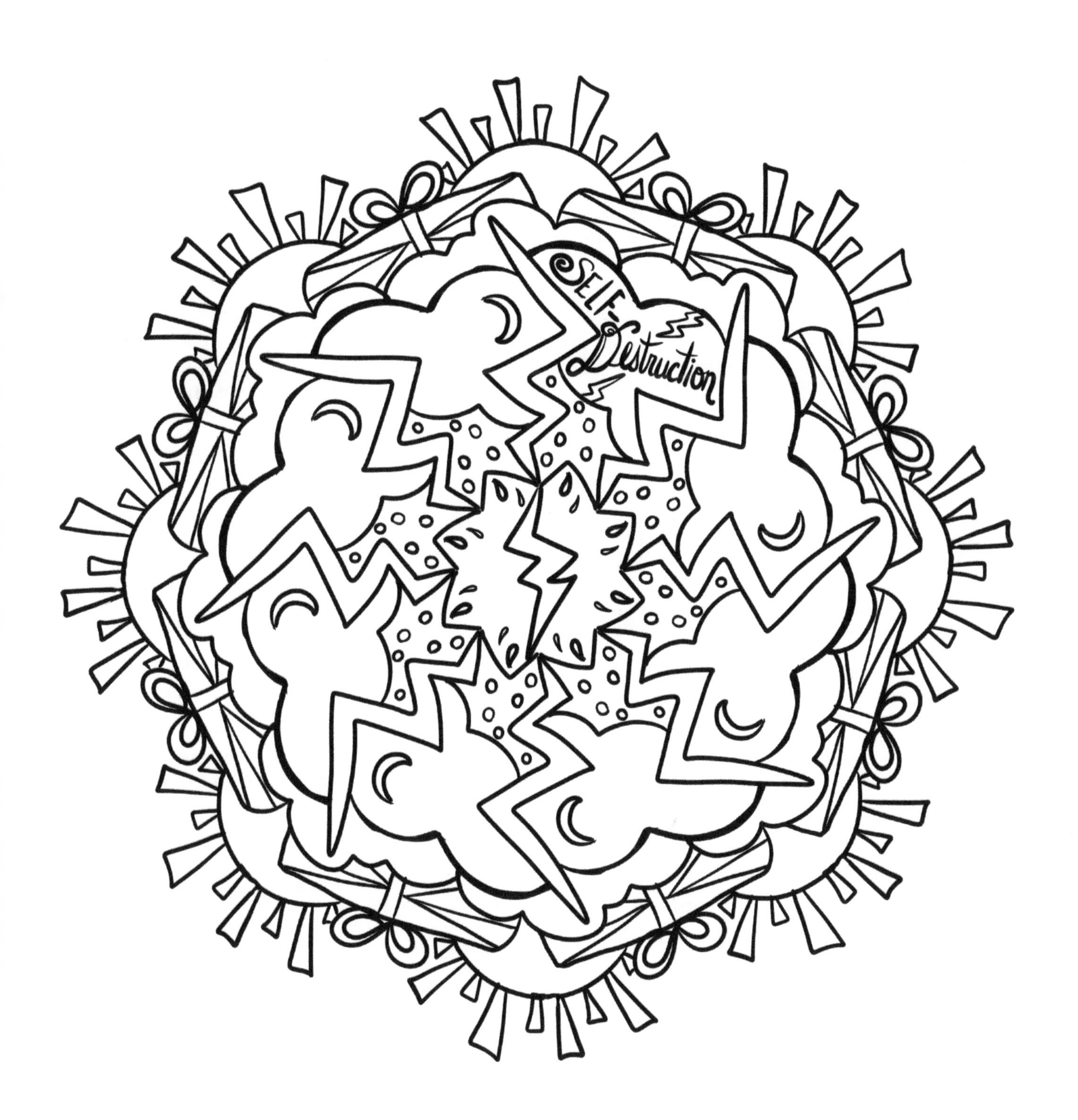
SELF-
Destruction

Self-Doubt

Self-Doubt is the Self-Wounding that second, third, and fourth guesses the wonderful gifts that make you uniquely you.

We all experience Self-Doubt, especially when we try to start something new and unfamiliar. A little Self-Doubt may do a great deal of good as we become open to learn and correct our mistakes. But too much will stifle us with deep insecurities and make us feel incapable of getting anywhere in life.

Self-Doubts are just your fears made manifest in order to protect you from humiliation and loss and keep you safe. They are the scared part of you that wants you to live small and stay safe by staying exactly the same. They are not the truth. They are fear-feasting stories you create about who you are, what you are capable of, and what you are worth. They often come from well-meaning family members, friends, teachers, and role models that think they are helping you see who you really are yet do quite the opposite. In fact, the best thing to do might be to doubt your doubts and call out that Saboteur voice and tell it that you are in charge now and know what is best.

Self-Doubt is one of the major obstacles to living the life you truly want for yourself. When you are full of Self-Doubt, you are more prone to making mistakes. It alters your thoughts in a way that distorts and deceives your truth. It destroys your heart with conflicting and false expectations and emotions from other people. It drags down your spirit by taking all the air out of your confidence and trust in yourself. It crushes the visions and dreams you have for yourself and prevents you from being and doing all you want to be and do.

Get rid of your Self-Doubt. Believe in yourself because no one else will if you don't. Overcome your Self-Doubt by looking at it from a new and fresh perspective of discovery and enthusiasm. See what it wants to show you about yourself. Be optimistic and claim your big and beautiful, full, and fabulous, powerful, and promising life. Be confident and committed to who you are and what you have to offer the world. Never let self-doubt hold you back in life. Stop the second, third, and fourth guessing and instead, step out of your comfort zone and try new things that will help you become a better version of yourself. You are worthy of all you dream and hope for!

I am proud of who I am and trust in my abilities to live life fully.

I have the power to do anything I put my mind to.

I refuse to doubt what I know to be true about myself.

"You can either waltz boldly onto the stage of life and live the way you know your spirit is nudging you to, or you can sit quietly by the wall, receding into the shadows of self-doubt." –Oprah Winfrey

"The worst enemy to creativity is self-doubt." –Sylvia Plath

"If you don't have some self-doubts and fears when you pursue a dream, then you haven't dreamed big enough." –Joe Vitale

MEPSS Activities

Mental – Have a 'doubt off.' Bring a doubt to mind and say,' I doubt it.' Listen to the reply and then say 'I doubt it' again. Continue until you find yourself laughing at the ridiculousness of its claim and send it away with the new truth you discovered instead.

Emotional – Find a family photo or a photo of someone whose voice still causes you to doubt yourself. Look at their picture and tell them, "Thank you for your role in my life and learning. I am now a capable adult and can live my life successfully the way I choose."

Physical – Imagine yourself as a superhero; anyone you like or make up one of your own with all the qualities you want to include. Then, imagine putting on your special powers and sense the self-doubt fall away, disintegrate, and disappear as you transform into your powerful, confident superhero self. Take a powerful stance, and experiment with bodily postures and expressions until you can feel your superpowers taking over. Speak your power, show it to the world, and celebrate the good you have brought to all who have self-doubt in the world. Have fun with this and if you like, dress up, take a selfie and share it. Or make a drawing or painting, or collage or sculpture of it and put it somewhere visible so that you can transform easily into your superhero when need be.

Social – Combat 'imposter syndrome'* by reading this modified Marianne Williamson* quote to yourself. Make a copy of it and post it in places around your house where you can say it over and over again until you have it memorized.

"My deepest fear is not that I am inadequate. My deepest fear is that I am powerful beyond measure. It is my light, not my darkness that most frightens me. I ask myself, who am I to be brilliant, gorgeous, talented, fabulous? Actually, who are you not to be? You are a child of God. Your playing small does not serve the world. There is nothing enlightened about shrinking so that other people won't feel insecure around you.

Spiritual – Imagine yourself as a stained-glass window that sparkles and shines when the sun is out, knowing that when the darkness sets in that your true beauty is revealed only if there is light from within. Name and claim that light and let it shine through all you are and all you do. If you are unsure whether or not you have this light of illumination within, ask for it from whatever source greater and beyond you that you feel comfortable with asking. Then be open to receiving it and offering gratitude and appreciation once you sense its presence, guidance, and light.

SELF-DOUBT

Self-Effacing

Self-Effacing is the Self-Wounding that uses camouflage to diminish the gifts of your bigger, bolder, want-to-be-seen self.

Self-Effacing behaviors are used to downplay your beautiful, unique self as a sort of false humility, meekness, modesty, or reserve to not draw attention to all you are in your magnificence. In many cultures, it is shrouded in modesty to reduce the social risk of offending others.

When engaged in Self-Effacing behaviors, you may feel awkward and shy and not speak much in social situations. You prefer to avoid social situations altogether and may have trouble reaching out for connection. You may have a hard time speaking up about your achievements, ideas, and stories because you don't feel you deserve to be heard or appreciated. Instead, you try to keep the focus on others, so you don't have to respond, or if you do respond, you do so with short, awkward, or terse replies or make not-so-funny jokes at your own expense. You may feel incompetent or inadequate and have trouble receiving attention and compliments gracefully. Instead, you deflect, play them down, or become a buffoon and let people laugh at you.

When you are Self-Effacing, diminish, doubt, and under-represent your skills, abilities, talents, and traits, you lose Self-Confidence, which can be a self-made obstacle to achieving your goals. Others may see this as aloof. Or others may distrust your competence, effectiveness, and your quality of contribution. It also makes it harder for women to be seen as smart, capable, competent, and able to take on the tasks required of men. When you engage in Self-Effacing behaviors, the damage is compounded because it sabotages all of you in the process.

Self-Effacing people are secretly confident; it is just buried deep inside. You must take off the camouflage, let yourself be seen, begin to stand out, become noticeable, and be confident in your bigger, bolder, want-to-be-seen self.

I have so much to contribute.

I speak up and share my ideas and opinions easily and effortlessly.

I welcome compliments as the truth they are.

"To reach perfection, we must all pass, one by one, through the death of self-effacement." –Dag Hammarskjold

"Ask yourself this: How much deprivation, how much self-effacement must you suffer through before you act on your desire for meaning and fulfillment? Before it's your turn to thrive in your life, instead of barely surviving it? Some people live their dreams. Why not you?" –Jillian Michaels

"Women are always self-effacing and self-denying. There's a term that enrages me, and I always used to swear that I'd never play characters described that way. The term is 'long-suffering.'" –Helen Mirren

MEPSS Activities

Mental – Challenge yourself to stop negative, Self-Effacing self-talk. List 5 situations or places where you are Self-Effacing. See if you can figure out what thoughts and reasons you tell yourself. List 3 of them, then counter those reasons with reasons from your bigger, bolder, want to be seen self.

Emotional – List 3 ways you downplay your worth with Self-Effacing behaviors. Then go ahead and exaggerate them until they feel absurd. If you want, you can record yourself doing this as long as you bring a sense of lightness and play to it. Then, instead of exaggerating or diminishing each of the 3, find a balance between the two extremes and practice this new healthy and helpful way of being.

Physical – Throw a party with you as the only guest. Instead of being Self-Effacing and shy, imagine or pretend to take credit for your accomplishments as your bigger, bolder, want-to-be-seen self being happy for what you have achieved. You can throw imaginary or real confetti or anything you want to make the celebration real for you. In this spirit of this place, set 3 big and exciting goals. List the first step you will take for each and work towards them. Write an invitation for your next party and plan your celebration as your bigger, bolder, want-to-be-seen self.

Social – Imagine yourself as a leader practicing assertiveness. How will you hold your body and posture*? What will you say? What tone and tenor will you use? What else will you do to show that you are the leader? If you want, draw a caricature of you in this leadership role. Post it somewhere you will see it often and refer to it when you are called to lead. When you put yourself first, you are in the best position to help others.

Spiritual – Sometimes, when you are silent, Self-Effacing, and attentive, you attract others who see you as someone they can share confidences with. Is this something that happens to you? Do you like it? If so, imagine yourself in a listening situation. How do you show kindness and compassion through your demeanor, expressions, postures, gestures, and nonverbal communication? If not, list some ways you can try to avoid the situation.

Self
Effacing

Self-Flattery

Self-Flattery is the fluttery-eyed Self-Wounding that overcompensates when receiving the gift of a compliment.

Self-Flattery is a lighthearted lie that exaggerates and praises your achievements while glossing over or denying your weaknesses or failings. The motive is to further your interests by 'sucking up' to someone in the hopes of receiving a compliment or favor, but instead, it becomes a form of manipulation that sets you up for failure when you can't live up to the claims you've just made about yourself and don't get what you used Self-Flattery for in the first place. It can weaken love and be used to abuse yourself and others.

Self-Flattery is compensation for low Self-Esteem, thinking you must somehow be better than you believe yourself to be. It activates your pride, which will stir you to commit actions that aren't planned well or are healthy for the situation or your overall life.

Self-Flattery is dishonest when used to gain control and can lead to dangerous places in relationships. It is effective because everyone has insecurities and loves to receive compliments and be told great things about themselves. It is often used in dating and relationships to get what you want. It is also commonly used in the workplace to place yourself above another in the hopes of receiving a promotion or other perks. Parents, especially mothers, may use Self-Flattery to show off their parenting skills. Self-Flattery is exciting in the moment but can lead to dangerous places. It can eventually make you feel annoyed or resentful as you continue to devalue your unique gifts, talents, and skills.

Self-Flattery is a cheap way of improving your image. It tells others that you are trying to take the easy route towards improving your image but only through words rather than working hard to attain and maintain the positive image you desire.

Instead, ask yourself why you feel an urge to subtly compliment yourself. What is the need underneath that needs to be met in another, healthier way? In this way, Self-Flattery is vital because it helps you figure out who you want to become based on your or another's response. It's a subtle form of a compliment that allows you to feel good internally in the moment. It can motivate you to instill generosity, intelligence, and wisdom in yourself. It can help you change your perception of yourself to one humbler, modest, more truthful, and able to receive the gift of a compliment without all the fluttery-eyed wounding.

I express myself freely, confidently, and truthfully.
I love and accept myself exactly as I am.
I accept compliments with ease and grace.

"Flattery is like chewing gum. Enjoy it, but don't swallow it."
–Hank Ketcham

'Self-flattery has a short battery life, but reminding yourself that you are amazing and precious and wanted and works of art can truly change your life.' –Donald Miller

'I believe that love not imitation is the sincerest form of flattery. Your imitator thinks that you can be duplicated, your lover knows you cannot.' –Marilyn Vos Savant

MEPSS Activities

Mental – What area is the easiest for you to succumb to Self-Flattery? Make a list of your talents and what people appreciate about you in that particular area. Then give yourself a 'sticky star' for each one and post it in your room. If you want more 'stars,' do the same for other areas.

Emotional – What Self-Flattering half-truths do you tell yourself? Choose 1 or 2 and ask yourself, 'What would the whole truth be?' Go deeper and ask yourself, 'What need* is underneath this false truth that wants to be filled?' Choose something that satisfies and meets this need in a healthier way.

Physical – Practice giving yourself realistic compliments. Write a list of compliments, cut them into slips of paper with one on each, then read one each day in front of the mirror. Do something simple for yourself to acknowledge and accept the compliment.

Social – Take a look at your close relationships. Ask yourself – Which relationships threaten me somehow and make me want to elevate myself above them? Go through 2 or 3 looking closer, and ask, 'What is an underlying motive in the relationship that makes me uncomfortable as I am? What can I change to be fully my true self?'

Spiritual – Learn to praise yourself for who you truly are as a beloved human being by seeing yourself through the eyes and heart of a Benevolent Divine Source of Love that knows you intimately. Find a picture that expresses you as this beloved, praise-worthy cherished person. Keep it somewhere you can look at it whenever you want or need to.

SELF
FLATTERY

Self-Gratification

Self-Gratification is the indulgent, kid in the candy store Self-Wounding that substitutes for the gift of pleasing yourself in a moderate, reasonable, and healthy way.

Self-Gratification is the act of satisfying one's desires, needs, or impulses. It's a natural human instinct to want pleasurable things and to want them now. You are tempted to indulge in the moment, using a 'quick fix' because it makes you feel good. Self-Gratification can be done in a variety of ways and has many consequences for your health and well-being.

The problem with Self-Gratification is that it only leads to short-term relief. When done impulsively, your brain's pathways for that action are reinforced and strengthened, making it easier to fall into the same pattern of craving again and again and harder to break the cycle. It can become an unhealthy pattern that leads to addiction to pornography or other substances, behavioral problems, health issues, and continued frustration from not having your deepest needs met properly. It becomes a serious issue when the addiction becomes stronger over time. Making it stop is difficult, if not impossible, without some form of medical help or intervention.

Delaying Self-Gratification takes a considerable effort, resulting in energy depletion. It isn't an easy skill to acquire because it initially involves feeling dissatisfied. And our world relies on this dissatisfaction to trigger instant Self-Gratification for just about everything – from likes on social media to food, entertainment, online shopping, and even dating. These and more are designed to make it easy for you to obtain whatever you want instantly, but it still may not feel fast enough!

Yet the ability to delay gratification can be lifesaving. A delay allows you to create strategies to understand your impulses and stop them in time to make better choices and consider long-term rewards as you continue to practice them. When you see how long-term goals are beneficial for your success over the short-term rewards of instant Self-Gratification and learn how to manage your need to be satisfied in the moment, you will thrive in your career, finances, health, and relationships, and you will contribute to a happier, healthier world.

Instead of acting from that 'kid in the candy store' place of indulgence, find new ways to take care of yourself; be kinder, more patient, and spend time on activities that make you happy and feel fulfilled. These gifts of pleasing yourself in a moderate, reasonable, and healthy way connect you to Self-Wonderfuls such as Self-Awareness, Self-Control, and Self-Discipline as well as Self-Care, Self-Regard, Self-Reflection, and Self-Worth and are the best treat you can give yourself!

I am patient and proactive, and I accept that I cannot always have what I want instantly.

I achieve my best life by taking the time, effort, and perseverance.

I offer myself pleasure in moderate, reasonable, and healthy ways.

"Many persons have the wrong idea of what constitutes true happiness. It is not attained through self-gratification but through fidelity to a worthy purpose." –Helen Keller

"Love is a many-sided sacrifice; it means thoughtfulness for others; it means putting their good before self-gratification. Love is impulse no doubt, but true love is impulse wisely directed." –Hugh Reginald Haweis

"For me, self-gratification eventually took a back seat to trying to do something collaborative with other people, to trying to make something new." –Ariel Pink

MEPSS Activities

Mental – One way to cultivate healthy Self-Gratification is by turning your thoughts in another direction or blocking those thoughts you don't want to think about. Spend time thinking about your future, what you want to achieve long-term, and what sort of person you want to be in the future. Read a book, learn a new language, or learn new information in a category you find interesting to help reach your future vision of yourself.

Emotional – Mourning allows you to express the grief of loss you have suffered and can lead to unhealthy Self-Gratification behaviors. Listening to music is one of the best ways to delay Self-Gratification. Take time today to listen to a piece of music that allows you to express your emotions in a way that offers you the beauty of the circle of life and death.

Physical – Pushing yourself out of your comfort zone by exercising is a fantastic way of giving you that happy feeling even after your workout. What type of exercise will you commit to today? You can do this alone or with others. To support your exercise, eat a healthy meal and forego fast food.

Social – Have fun today noticing what our society says you need to 'feel good' and the special status that results from doing or having something like wearing the latest fashion trend, driving a fancy car, owning a status symbol, dining at 5-star restaurants, taking a luxurious cruise or vacation, or even attending an elite school. Which ones have you dreamt of? What would it give you? And for how long?

Spiritual – Having a spiritual practice or vital practice* opens you up to the gifts the Universe offers and becomes a bridge between being and doing. Begin a spiritual practice of prayer, meditation, or reverential dance. Or begin meeting with people who grow your soul as a kind of transcendent pleasure and relief from stress, your own selfish desires, and Self-Gratification. Explore where 'sin'* or 'missing the mark'* keeps you from claiming your divine nobility in the lineage of love and blocks your search for Absolute Truth and true happiness.

Self-Gratification

Self-Harm

Self-Harm is the toolbox of sharp, hurtful objects used for purposeful, pseudo-pleasurable Self-Wounding that cuts away at the gifts of loving and accepting yourself.

Self-Harm is a way of dealing with deep distress and emotional pain. There is often a connection to childhood trauma. It is the intentional, direct injuring of your own body without suicidal intentions. It can be a way to stop feeling numb or disconnected, express pain and intense darker feelings you can't express verbally, release tension or vent anger, and distract you from your life when you just don't know what else to do. It can also be a way to calm and soothe yourself, which might help you feel better for a while, but when the painful feelings, anxiety, and tension return, you will have the urge to hurt yourself again.

Self-Harm includes anything you do intentionally to physically injure yourself. This includes cutting yourself with scissors or a razor, burning, scratching, bruising, carving words, or symbols into your skin, banging your head against a wall, punching, pinching, binge-eating, food-restricting, hair-pulling, drinking to excess, abusing legal or illegal substances, self-isolation, and many more. An extreme form of Self-

Abuse is self-flagellation or whipping yourself as punishment.

Self-Harm is an attempt to deal with a sense that you need to suffer, that you are supposed to suffer and that suffering will make you a better person, but it does not resolve the issue that made you want to hurt yourself in the first place. You step in and become the parent to yourself and punish yourself for not measuring up with the harmful ways you learned in childhood and see others use now. You are directing emotional expression on yourself rather than externalizing and directing them toward others.

People who Self-Harm believe that physical pain can take away emotional pain and can create a sense of calm and relief. The brain starts to connect the relief from emotional pain with the Self-Harm. As a result, a pleasure/pain loop is created, releasing endorphins to make you feel better. With a little bit of pain, you get immediate results. These acts of self-abuse can then become a craving that can be difficult to resist and become addictive as you rely on the boost the endorphins provide. Self-Harm becomes a trap because each time you do it, you need more to obtain the same good feelings and mood, and the cycle continues.

To stop Self-Harm, it's important to match the solution to the reason for Self-Harm. You must begin to accept that there are more effective ways to overcome the underlying issues that drive your Self-Harm and that you can handle feeling darker emotions for a while. As you experience feeling better sooner than expected, you begin building emotional resilience. Another way to stop self-harm is having friends who make you feel worthy and cared for or being in a loving relationship that promotes your spiritual well-being and happiness and cares for you in a safe, supportive way. And sometimes, you simply grow out of it and don't have the need anymore!

Self-Harm can be very difficult to stop on your own. If you are struggling with Self-Harm, reaching out to a mental health professional* for support, help, and accountability is important. They are there to help and want to help, so you can begin to enhance the Self Wonderfuls of Self-Acceptance, Self-Esteem, Self-Love, Self-Respect, and Self-Worth and learn to love and accept yourself again.

I have suffered more than enough in my life.
I offer myself kindness and love now.
I can love myself by standing up for what is right for me without harming myself.

"My words of encouragement for teen girls suffering with an eating disorder, self-harm, anything... is to get help. It's the most important thing you can do for yourself, and it can change your life and potentially save your life." –Demi Lovato

'Never feel this bad again. Never come back to this place, where only a knife will do. Live a gentle and kind life. Don't do things that make you want to self-harm. Whatever you do, every day, remember this – then steer away from here.' –Caitlin Moran

"Be honest. Don't hide. Healing is possible, and there is a way to feel real and alive without self-harming." –Chelsie Skroback

MEPSS Activities

Mental – Understanding what triggers you to Self-Harm is vital to recovery. Make a list of situations and circumstances that you engage in before you have the desire to Self-Harm. What criticisms, judgments, or emotions are you trying to deal with in those situations and circumstances? What does your Saboteur's voice say to you? What is false about it? Why do you believe it?

Emotional – When you feel intense emotions, instead of Self-Harming, listen to music that expresses what you are feeling. Move your body to express the music's beat, passion, and intensity in big and bold ways. As the intense emotions start to subside, notice the new ones that show up and let those be expressed. Don't think about it or attach a story or thought; just let yourself move and be moved!

Physical – If you Self-Harm to calm and soothe yourself, try soothing yourself and your body with some pampering. Take a hot shower or bubble bath. As you are soaking, massage your neck, hands, and feet. Light a candle, and listen to soft, calming music. When you get out, wrap yourself in a comfy, warm blanket and give yourself a big hug.

Social – If you often get angry or need to release tension when out with others in a social setting, carry a soft 'stress ball' that you can squeeze in your pocket. Squeeze it hard and make up a rhythm to focus on, perhaps to match your breathing or the music's beat.

Spiritual – When you feel disconnected or numb, remind yourself that you are never alone. Compose a poem or song to your most cherished self as you know it to be deep inside your heart, beyond any criticism, pain, trauma, doubt, or disbelief. If you want, record it so you can play it back to yourself when you have the urge to Self-Harm.

Self-Harm

Self-Humiliation

Self-Humiliation is the Self-Wounding that keeps lowering the price on the gift of the priceless, creative, uniquely you before others can.

Self-Humiliation is a quick way to disapprove of yourself before another person humiliates you. It is associated with situations that do not show you in the best or even a helpful light and can cause embarrassment, anger, frustration, guilt, and shame. It's a way of diminishing yourself and your abilities based on the fear of rejection. If you are unhappy with yourself, there is a constant fear of failure that extends to relationships and even your work.

Everyone needs constant approval! It's a natural part of being human! You, like everyone else, grew up with those family members, friends, teachers, and colleagues who have been critical of you, and you believed, maybe not entirely, but in some way, that these criticisms, judgments, and appraisals of you were true and they have been internalized and simmer beneath the surface. They involve honor, status, and dignity, and if these criticisms are called out, especially in public, you are often left speechless and stunned. You want to hide, disappear, and become invisible. You become fearful that your status and standing have been sullied and your authority called into question. You may react by humiliating yourself to soften the blow. This is heightened when you are uncertain and cannot stand in your strengths and love for yourself. If you are secure and confident in yourself, you will rarely feel the shame of others' humiliation and can turn it back on them, knowing they are insecure and uncertain about who they are.

Self-Humiliation does not have to involve an act of aggression or coercion. You may take a more passive means and not speak up when you are ignored or overlooked, taken for granted, or denied a certain right or privilege, thus choosing to stay in a place of abuse, abandonment, betrayal, or reaction as a means to an end. Self-Humiliation is a way of denying your humanity. It is almost as if your heart shrivels as you undermine yourself and listen to that Saboteur's voice that feeds your insecurities and doubts.

When you stand up to your Saboteur's voice and counter it with the truth in love, you become the gift of the priceless, creative, uniquely you.

I let go of past humiliation and embrace all that I am.

I am a perfectly imperfect and worthwhile person.

My past actions do not define me in the present.

"Most acts of assent require far more courage than most acts of protest since courage is clearly a readiness to risk self-humiliation." –Nigel Dennis

"Know that humiliation does not weaken you; it strengthens you. The more egoistic you are, the more humiliation you feel. When you are childlike and have a greater sense of kinship, you do not feel humiliated. When you are steeped in love with the Existence, with the Divine, nothing whatsoever can humiliate you." –Sri Sri Ravi Shankar

"But self-abasement (self-humiliation) is just inverted egoism. Anyone who acts with genuine humility will be as far from humiliation as from arrogance." –Stephen Mitchell

MEPSS Activities

Mental – It becomes so easy to think Self-Humiliating thoughts as a proactive defense mechanism when needed. Unfortunately, they become truths you believe and act from. Think of a situation where you humiliated yourself and write down the Self-Humiliating phrases you used. Now, rephrase those words as empowerment mantras you can use next time.

Emotional – Self-Humiliation is often glorified and laughed at in movies and TV. Watch a favorite movie or TV series and put yourself in the scene of Self-Humiliation. What emotions and feelings did the scene evoke? How have these feelings hindered your growth and transformation? What will you change so that you support your true humility? What is the first step you will take?

Physical – Have fun and over-exaggerate a Self-Humiliating experience you have had. Think of those slapstick comic actors. Really play it up and get your whole body into it. Then make up a self-affirming version and exaggerate that as well. Notice how you feel after the second self-affirming version. Embrace that boldness and confidence and use it in the future to counter any temptation to deny your true self.

Social – Some people make you uncomfortable, and you sense that you have to put yourself down to connect with them. Make a list of those people. Then create some tactful phrases to tell yourself and reply to them that make avoiding them okay.

Spiritual – Self-Humiliation is a form of punishment, seen as a fate worse than death because it destroys your standing and your life. Take some time in a safe, comfortable place to reflect and perhaps journal on how your Self-Humiliation is similar to death and how it is different.

Self-
Humiliation

Self-Imposed

Self-Imposed is the Self-Wounding straitjacket you put on yourself that denies the gift of your full self-expression.

Self-Imposed attitudes and thoughts create your own barriers and limitations. In fact, all limits are Self-Imposed. The importance of this Self-Wounding is to remind you of the Self-Wonderful truth that the person you are and the person you will become has no limits, and with enough determination and focus, you can not only change anything about yourself but also achieve almost anything.

Most often, you create stress by putting limitations on yourself by interpreting an event in an unsupportive way. You internalize the descriptions and stories you and others tell you and ignore anything that doesn't match that perception of yourself. You view situations as all or nothing, dramatically magnify the unsupportive aspect of events, and catastrophize or come to an illogical conclusion about an event. Your mindset and the limiting beliefs you hold are often responsible for your lack of success. You cling to automatic phrases such as 'I can't,' 'I don't,' 'I won't,' or 'I should,' 'I must,' or 'I have to.' These Self-Imposed statements use blame, emotional reasoning, labeling, or overgeneralization to keep you from taking control of your life. When you restrict yourself, you guarantee you will never become anything more than you are now.

Instead of Self-Imposed actions, behaviors, and thoughts, be attentive to what passes through your mind and your reactions to them. Become the co-creator of your own life. Let go of the assumptions, comparisons, and stories you've made about yourself being unable to create your best life. Let go of how other people have tried to discourage and limit you. Even if you have made mistakes in the past, they don't define you. In fact, they can be your greatest teacher, and you are free to grow and change.

When you realize that you are the one who defines your limits and seek to stop Self-Imposed limits on yourself, you can do anything you set your mind to. You then let your authentic self, dreams, desires, values, and vision create the life you want and live the happiest and most inspired life you can imagine.

In a healthier way, Self-Imposed hardships can help you discover what you can do without and reduce your fear of losing things. They can also help you prepare for future hardships. Self-Imposed hardships can also increase your appreciation and enjoyment of the simpler things in life and help you better reflect upon your true goals in life. You can then take off the Self-Wounding straitjacket of a Self-Imposed life and live into the Self-Wonderful gift of your full self-expression.

I have the power to change the story and my life.

I choose to live big and bold as my true and authentic self.

I can do anything I put my mind and heart to and create the life I want.

"All the concepts about stepping out of your comfort zone mean nothing until you decide that your essential purpose, vision, and goals are more important than your self-imposed limitations." –Robert White

"Practice unfettered living from the heart, abandoning all self-imposed limitations to emerge anew, creativity unleashed, giving of yourself like never before." –Pooja Ruprell

"The genesis of exceptional living lives in the knowing that the boundary between your ideas and your acquisition of them can only be obscured by self-imposed barriers. Possibility is a state of being. Be about your life's big ideas." –LaShaun Middlebrooks Collier

MEPSS Activities

Mental – Put a fat rubber band on your wrist. Every time you think 'I can't,' 'won't,' 'should,' or 'try,' give the rubber band a flick, reminding you that you are having a Self-Imposing thought. Then match the Self-Imposing thought with a different thought you think will happen. Focus on the phrases you use and their impact and look out for the words. This way, when you anticipate something, you can make sure that you anticipate it wisely and diminish those Self-Imposing thoughts at the same time!

Emotional – Make a list of excuses you tell yourself that prevent you from having the life you want. Now, be your own motivational coach and write motivational statements for 5 of them, then do them. Give yourself a little incentive or reward afterward.

Physical – 20% of your tasks and activities are actually responsible for 80% of your desired outcomes. Use Self-Imposed limitations in a positive way in these areas: Write down the number of goals and tasks you accomplish and the amount of time they take to see big improvements in your focus, productivity, and success. Ask yourself, 'What one thing, if achieved today/this week/month/year, would lead me to consider today/this week/month/year to be a total success?' Then identify the first 5 most important steps that would significantly contribute toward achieving your one goal.

Social – Choose 5 people to surround yourself with who are more dedicated, hard-working, and more successful than you. Get to know them by observing and researching them for the day. Write down what they do that inspires you. Choose one of their inspiring actions to begin implementing in your life to shift your attitude and behaviors.

Spiritual – Here are some common acronyms for Fear: **F**uture **E**vents **A**lready **R**uined, **F**alse **E**vidence **A**ppearing **R**eal, **F**orget **E**verything and **R**un., and its counter: **F**ace **E**verything **A**nd **R**ise. What do you need to face in order to rise? Make a list of 20 things and choose one to face. Face it with Faith: **F**oundation **A**ssurance **I**ntegrity **T**rust **H**olding, in whatever way this looks for you.

Self-Imposed

Self-Indulgence

Self-Indulgence is the Self-Wounding avalanche of unrestrained actions that smothers and buries the gift of healthy living.

Everyone wants to have fun. You want to enjoy yourself, and satisfy your desires, whether they are seemingly small or must-haves. You may just want to be lazy, have no responsibilities, and do nothing all day. Sometimes you do need nurturing times of calm, rest, idleness, and recuperation, which is the healthy form of Self-Indulgence. It's the increasing amount and frequency that leads to unhealthy Self-Indulgence. Sometimes it happens with certain foods, television, movies, clothes, jewelry, expensive items, travel, bad language, anger, worry, sex, violence, or addictive substances. It can also be staying out too late with friends, partners, or lovers, even staying out in the sun too long, or putting your health and well-being at risk in other ways.

Self-Indulgence is doing exactly what you want when you want. It is focusing on yourself, your own pleasure, or comfort. It is having or wanting more than necessary or is required for health and life. It is impulsive and tries to feed your appetites, desires, passions, and whims in order to feel pleasure and satisfaction. When these actions take over and become habitual, they become an addiction and cause problems, either immediately or in the future.

Self-Indulgence feeds your dissatisfaction with life in unhealthy ways. You may be bored and weary from the everyday repetition of responsibilities, duties, obligations, and commitments, which cause restlessness and the desire for more pleasure and satisfaction. Fear may set in as you realize that life will always be this way. Failure can trigger Self-Indulgence when you realize that your dreams are not going to come true and you won't be able to achieve any significant goals.

Addictions start as Self-Indulgence. It brings other Self-Woundings to the surface: poor Self-Esteem, lack of Self-Respect, Self-Abuse, Self-Harm, and Self-Destruction.

To overcome excessive Self-Indulgence, many other Self-Wonderfuls can help: Self-Discipline, Self-Control, Self-Compassion, and Self-Understanding.

Sometimes it is very proactive to practice Self-Indulgence in nurturing ways that feed your heart and body. You are treating yourself to something that takes care of you, is loving and respectful, contributes to the gift of healthy living, and your continued growth toward transformation and Self-Actualization.

I take care of myself in a healthy, balanced, moderate way.

I adopt new strategies to cope with unpleasant thoughts and feelings.

I say no to Self-Indulgence.

"Live with hope and courage and love instead of a long season of whining, self-indulgence, and fear." –Shauna Niequist

"People need to understand that true happiness comes from self-development, not self-indulgence." –Jeffrey Fry

"Caring for myself is not self-indulgence, it is self-preservation, and that is an act of political warfare." –Audre Lorde

MEPSS Activities

Mental – The more thoughts we put into our outer pleasures and comforts, the less time we have to discover why we are really here. True happiness, fulfillment, and peace of mind will always be beyond your grasp. Take some solitary time today and indulge yourself, exploring the meaning of life through a book, article, or poem that is expansive and shimmers with what you want your unique life to represent.

Emotional – Choose one Self-Indulgent habit and ask yourself: What need* am I trying to fulfill with this habit? Then find a healthier way to meet this need. If you want to do more, by all means, indulge yourself in this healing practice!

Physical – What are 3 nurturing activities that can offer you the Self-Indulgence that take a minimum amount of time, effort, and money and feel satisfying and loving? It could be something as simple as preparing yourself your favorite beverage, taking an herb-scented bubble bath, or simply sitting in the sun or under a tree and enjoying nature's gifts.

Social – Is there someone in your life that you have crowded out as you have focused more on yourself? Think of a simple way to reach out to that person and give them some undivided attention. Then do it!

Spiritual – Your purpose in your earthly life is to learn about your spiritual destiny and how to achieve it. When you act from a place of nurturing Self-Indulgence, you become clearer about your true desires — qualities like fulfillment, happiness, service to others, and making the world and the people in it healthier and happier too! Spend 10 minutes contemplating what brings you pleasure on the grand scale of your purpose here on earth. Then narrow it down and get more specific until there is one easy action you can take today. Take that first action step and see what spiritual benefit it offers you. Enjoy this sensation of pleasure, delight, or emotional uplift. Do it again often!

Self-Indulgence

Self-Inflicted

Self-Inflicted is the Self-Woundings arrow you target yourself with that hurts the better choices to deal with your stress and pain.

Self-Inflicted wounding is something you bring upon yourself, whether it be unhealthy choices, harm to yourself, poor judgment, or something you cause to happen to you. Most often, it is Self-Inflicted stress from your behavioral or emotional responses to certain situations, often habitually ignored and unrecognized until great damage has been done.

Of course, Self-Inflicted wounding is a complex defense mechanism system that depends on various factors, including circumstances, unhealthy and unpleasant emotions, harmful thoughts, and personality tendencies. The key is always how you react in any given situation.

Often, you put pressure on yourself to perform or excel at something with unrealistic expectations or timeframes, then as the stress builds, you degrade and devalue yourself with critical, judgmental, or unsupportive thoughts that trigger unhealthy behaviors such as procrastination and emotions that then cascade into anxiety, depression, and Self-Inflicted actions that make you feel worse and worse about yourself and your abilities.

Self-Inflicted wounding can be stopped simply by waiting one minute before doing anything in reaction to what you are experiencing, feeling, or thinking. This gives you time to make a new, more healthy choice and a realistic way to motivate yourself to make the change you need to move forward in a more healthy, self-affirming way. This shift leads to access to many Self-Wonderfuls that can break the arrows you have shot at yourself and better support you in making new choices that spotlight the Simply Self-Wonderful YOU!

I am not defined by my past and forgive my past Self-Inflicted Woundings.

An incredible transformation is happening as I practice loving myself.

I am constantly growing and becoming a better person.

"Troubles hurt the most when they prove self-inflicted."
–Sophocles

"All pressure is self-inflicted. It's what you make of it or how you let it rub off on you." –Sebastian Coe

"Psychotherapy is what God has been secretly doing for centuries by other names; that is, God searches through our personal history and heals what needs to be healed – the wounds of childhood or our own self-inflicted wounds."
–Thomas Keating

MEPSS Activities

Mental – So many of our Self-Inflicted Woundings come from the conversations we have in our mind that wants the best for you but tries to do it from a place of judging and shaming. This is always a lie and never works! List 10 things you tell yourself before you act on a Self-Inflicted wounding. Now change those Self-Wounding thought statements into Self-Wonderful statements adding the alternate, healthier actions you will take to practice a new way of loving yourself.

Emotional – Try the 60-second technique* or 'passing clouds'* practice and simply be aware of the emotions passing through your body. Simply let them move through without attaching a belief, story, or thought to them. Just wait. It's that simple. Hit the pause button, and don't do anything! Be patient with yourself; this is new and powerful and requires practice for the rest of your life! When you attach a belief, story, or thought to them, simply offer yourself self-compassion and notice where the emotion has attached to your body. Then simply make an intention to drain that area by dropping the emotional energy back into the earth, for when charged psychic energy enters the forcefield of the earth, it is neutralized. Congratulate yourself, and notice the freedom and new energy you feel!

Physical – List 3 ways you create Self-Inflicted Woundings in your everyday life. What are the results when you stall or procrastinate? Choose one of the 3 Self-Inflicted Woundings you have listed and redo the situation to prevent yourself from feeling overwhelmed and incapable in the future. Start at the beginning and take it 'one step at a time.' What would a healthy, productive first step be? Taking the first step can be the hardest, but when you do, it gives you the momentum (and success) to take a second and third and more until you reach completion. What would a second and third step be? Celebrate yourself after each step. You can do this! And the good news is that it will become easier and easier each time you do!

Social – Perhaps you know someone with a Self-Inflicted Wounding, an addiction to harmful substances, drugs, eating disorders, gambling, or even excessive shopping. Rather than help them help yourself by learning what you can say and do to encourage them to begin their healing process. It's a wonderful way to be a concerned and supportive friend and offer yourself new gifts of compassion, insight, and healing!

Spiritual – What does your spiritual tradition say about healing your childhood wounds or your own Self-Inflicted wounds? What comfort and solace do they give? What practices do they offer? If you have felt a lack of support or distance from your tradition, or if you don't have a spiritual tradition of choice, do some internet research, and make inquiries with one that resonates with you. Remember that spiritual traditions are human-made traditions, practices, and worldviews that point to the great, indescribable mystery we all experience at one time or another and can support us throughout life whether we believe it or not.

Self-
Inflicted

Self-Involved

Self-Involved is the Self-Wounding that watches the movie of yourself over and over again in your own private theater, refusing a ticket to the gift of another's company.

Self-Involved is being wrapped up in your own thoughts and concerns with your own desire, interests, or needs and is preoccupied with unhealthy Self-Love. When you are Self-Involved, you only see reflections of yourself. You see others existing only as shadows and fail to see or have an awareness, compassion, or understanding for other people and their wants and needs.

When you are Self-Involved, you often self-reference yourself in interactions with others, so the focus stays on you. You fail to be curious, complimentary, interested, or even notice or register anything about them because it's all about you. In truth, you have a great need for love yet cannot depend on anyone because of your deep distrust and depreciation of others. Your behavior is often boastful, controlling, grandiose, and even haughty, and you use this as a defense against needing others. As with all the Self-Woundings, this goes back to a childhood deprivation resulting in a wounding behavior that can be healed and become a gift.

A Self-Involved person often is seen as a loner and superficial, and the common label these days is 'narcissistic.' You believe you are better than others and focus on power and status in an exaggerated or unhealthy way. You don't care about other people or what other people tell you. The world revolves around you, and you pay no attention to what others are doing or saying. You don't get involved and prefer interacting with your electronic devices over a real, living human being.

Yet, some of these things can just mean that you value your time and are self-aware. You have a level-headed approach and are open-minded. You are loyal to your friends and may have less of a need for peer acceptance than most people. You can still be charming and charismatic and have some social interactions, but they don't matter as much. You set clear boundaries and are not codependent. You still care and may be deeply empathetic to the point that it actually hurts you to be around others. You are deeply intuitive and, together with empathy, this may be why you focus on yourself as a means of protection from those deep feelings and sensations that you are uncomfortable with deep inside you.

Being Self-Involved requires balance. You want to pay attention to yourself, your needs, and your wants and be present and available for others. It's just fine to watch the movie of yourself over and over again in your own private theater, as long as you buy a ticket of the gift of another's company and watch the movie of them too.

I pay attention to myself in a balanced and healthy way.

I enjoy the company of others.

I take pleasure in the simple things in life.

'Now don't please, be quite so single-minded, self-involved, or assume the world is wrong and you are right. Whoever thinks that they alone possess intelligence, the gift of eloquence, they and no one else, and character too… such people, I tell you, spread them open, and you will find them empty.' –Antigone

"Kindness is something that I feel is leaving us a little bit – people are getting more self-involved." –Cobie Smulders

"Adolescents, for all their self-involvement, are emerging from the self-centeredness of childhood. Their perception of other people has more depth. They are better equipped at appreciating others' reasons for action or the basis of others' emotions. But this maturity functions in a piecemeal fashion. They show more understanding of their friends, but not of their teachers." –Terri E Apter

MEPSS Activities

Mental – Indulge yourself by going to a public place and people-watch. Notice your thoughts. Do you start telling yourself stories about others or compare yourself in a superior way? What are 5 thoughts that are repeated over and over again? Go deeper and ask, What are the needs* beneath those thoughts? How can you meet 2 of those needs in a more supportive way for yourself? Take the first step to meet the chosen needs.

Emotional – Make a list of 7 ways to love* yourself in a genuinely caring way. Choose one to do each day this week. Go all out and really feel the love.

Physical – Pleasure is Self-Involved. Treat yourself to a pleasurable experience. Simply get caught up in the experience and enjoy it. Notice the difference it makes in all areas of your life.

Social – Choose two people to pay attention to today. Observe their lives, not as a stalker, of course, but with curiosity and interest in what they do and say, who they are, and how they express themselves. How self-involved are they? How involved with others are they? Just notice with no judgment the life of another person.

Spiritual – Spend some quiet time reflecting on your motivation for doing something to benefit others. What's in it for you? Now choose a similar activity to do simply for the doing of it, letting go of caring whether it will be of use or not. What differences did you notice when you did it from a place of nonattachment? What similarities did you notice?

What does this tell you about yourself?

SELF-
involved

Self-Judgment

Self-Judgment is the Self-Wounding that brings the gavel down, declaring your critical opinions of yourself as true while failing to acquit the gifts of your goodness and worth.

Self-Judgment is the view you take of yourself as you rate your qualities by various standards. Self-Judgment is a learned behavior. You form opinions that may or may not be accurate or true. Your opinions reinforce how you feel about yourself. The truth is that you are your own worst judge. The goal is to lessen the critical ones and increase the ones that affirm who you are.

Once you start to accept inaccurate or faulty thoughts about yourself, your ability to see yourself realistically becomes clouded. Then you start paying attention to what provides evidence for these inaccurate or faulty beliefs. But the real truth is that all those unhealthy and toxic words, all those feelings that make you feel like something is wrong with you, are just lies.

Then on top of this, you judge yourself for judging yourself! Other Self-Woundings jump into action. Self-Judgment and Self-Criticism are Self-Defeating and are ineffective tools for self-improvement. It is Self-Defeating to attempt nonjudgment by telling yourself that judgmental thoughts are bad and then judging and criticizing yourself for it!

Self-Judgment is just a 'mind virus' that you caught from some unhealthy person or environment. And although it feels personal, it is not! It blinds you to the actual causes and prevents you from seeking solutions. The truth is that you are infinitely valuable, worthy, and enough.

Instead of Self-Judgment, be yourself. Remove yourself from the courtroom, throw away the gavel, and give yourself the gifts of your goodness and worth. Use the many Self-Wonderful gifts to accept and love yourself just as you truly are.

I am nonjudgmental of myself and others.
I refuse to be affected by the judgment of others.
I see myself accurately and embrace the gift of me.

"Remember, you have been judging yourself for years, and it hasn't worked. Try approving of yourself and see what happens." –Louise L. Hay

"Transform your world by transforming your inner state. Start by learning to let go of negative self-judgment and replace it with positive and loving thoughts about yourself. Be kind to yourself and watch your external world change." –Anita Moorjani

"Do not carry the burden of self-judgment. You are forgiven and pardoned." –Sunday Adelaja

MEPSS Activities

Mental – Commit yourself to ignore (give no value to) any thought, word, feeling, or behavior not in alignment with Self-Love and Self-Empowerment. Thank this Saboteur* for its previous service and tell it that you have learned a new way. Choose a new voice to listen to; perhaps one that is an archetype that can offer you wisdom, truth, and love. Find a symbol or picture to remind you of this new way of being.

Emotional – Ask yourself – what would my life be like if I were free from Self-Judgment? How would I feel? What shifts happen as you are fully present in this mind experience of freedom? Then identify one small phrase or action that can bring you back to this reminder in a moment of choice.

Physical – Each time you find yourself judging one of your body parts today, tell that body part this phrase, '(Body part), you are powerful, valuable and lovable just as you are, and I am grateful for your continued service in my life,' then give yourself a big hug.

Social – Pick a day, and every time you are aware that you are judging yourself, put a quarter in a jar. Count up what you have and put the money toward doing something loving for someone else. Continue to do this each day for a month and see what a difference it makes in your life and the life of the person or organization you chose to donate to.

Spiritual – For this practice, you will need to collect some small stones that you can hold in the palm of your hand. You will also need a bowl that can hold the stones about halfway full and a pitcher with enough water to cover the stones. Take one stone in your left palm and name one Self-Judgment you hold. Really feel the hurt, pain, and suffering it has caused you throughout your life. When you've had enough (and don't stay here too long), transfer the stone to your right palm and offer it forgiveness* by saying, 'I forgive myself for________.' Then place that stone in the bowl of water. Continue with each stone until you feel you have covered enough for now. Then pour water over all the stones in the bowl, cleansing, healing, and restoring your ability to love yourself. Keep the bowl of stones covered in water as long as you wish to remind yourself that forgiveness is always available. Return the stones to where you found them when you feel this ritual is complete.

SELF-
JUDGMENT

Self-Licensing

Self-Licensing is the Self-Wounding that looks in the rearview mirror without guilt that refuses to drive using the gifts of better judgment and consideration.

Self-Licensing is a way that you self-regulate your moral or ethical behavior. Self-Licensing, at its core, is an identity crisis. It shows that there is a discrepancy or inconsistency between your behaviors, feelings, and thoughts, which can lead to a wide range of self-justified undesirable behaviors. It's a kind of psychological bargaining you use to fool yourself to justify 'bad' behavior using other 'good' behaviors, although the terms 'good' and 'bad' are not helpful ways to label your behavior.

Self-Licensing can range from rewarding yourself with unhealthy food and beverages, expensive items, forgoing your diet and exercising, splurging, and sabotaging your efforts at something you want to achieve or have but lack the willpower to do in a healthy or moral way. It can also be seen abusing others, bigotry, cheating, discrimination, financial contributions, harassment, off-color jokes, lying, prejudice, procrastination, racism, substance abuse, stereotyping, taking shortcuts, and anything else you use to justify your Self-Licensing behavior. The sneakiest trick of Self-Licensing is being ignorant about the effect.

Ultimately, Self-Licensing has nothing to do with vice or virtue or as a test of your character. Rather, Self-Licensing sidesteps your commitment to achieving your dreams and goals and becomes a trap of Self-Sabotage. Anyone can fall victim to giving themselves excuses, so make sure that instead, you drive using your front-view mirror gifts of better judgment and consideration to achieve your dreams and goals and flourish in life.

I act with integrity and purpose to reach my dreams and goals.

I am valued for who I am, not what I do.

I believe in my highest self and want to act in favor of that self.

"Personal liberty is not personal license." –Billy Sunday

"The imagination, give it the least license, dives deeper and soars higher than Nature goes." –Henry David Thoreau

"So much of the habitat destruction and pollution is based on the simple principle that we somehow have been given free license over other species to degrade the planet." –Greg Graffin

MEPSS Activities

Mental – What is one way you have repeatedly acted with Self-License? What outcomes did your actions create? Was the behavior you displayed in line with your Self-Image and the person you dream of becoming? If not, write the new outcomes you want your actions to create.

Emotional – Think of a time when you felt like you were right, became bossy, and acted with Self-License to make sure that you got your way. How did that feel? Take time to write and explore the underlying motivations for your behavior. What did you get out of it? Take time to reflect on how you might do it differently next time to make sure you get your needs met.

Physical – Make a list of 15 times you used past healthy behavior to justify indulging. The 3 biggest ones are exercise and weight loss, health and well-being, and finances. Pause and recall 3 of those times and remember why you participated in that healthy behavior in the first place. Why are these goals important to you? Practice the 5-fold way by answering the 'why' question 5 times, going deeper into each item to get to the very bottom of why this goal is meaningful to you. Do this for each of the 3 times.

1. Why do you want to (name of healthy behavior) in the first place?
2. Why do you want to (answer to Q1) ?
3. Why do you want to (answer to Q2)?
4. Why do you want to (answer to Q3)?
5. Why do you want to (answer to Q4)?

What have you learned about your motivation and behavior that you can use to help you make healthy choices for the right reasons in the future?

Social – Climate change is one area where nearly all agree that something needs to be done now. What specific area will you make a bold stand in and engage others? What commitment statement will you make to keep you active and engaged? What will your first step be today to honor that commitment?

Spiritual – Choose a religious tradition and explore the ways that followers of that religion have acted with Self-License to enforce the moral and ethical behavior they ascribe to. How have these helped the faithful? How have these harmed the faithful? How have these been imposed on those outside the religious tradition? How have they been opposed or pushed back on by those outside the religious tradition? What do you think the underlying moral or ethical principle is? What are some ways to encourage them that are less harmful and offensive?

Or, using these same questions, how have you acted with Self-License to insist that others follow the moral and ethical behavior you ascribe to?

LICENSING
Self-Self-Self-Self-Self-Self-Self-Self-

Self-Loathing

Self-Loathing is the cavernous Self-Wounding black hole that denies the light of the gift of your wonderfulness.

Self-Loathing is that underlying feeling that you are inadequate, not good enough at something or anything. It can be subtle, yet it creates a deep hole of criticism, blame, shame, fault-finding, scolding, and even prejudice that constantly berates you and tells you how stupid, insensitive, or embarrassing you are. It is synonymous with self-hatred. And it simply isn't true! You are worthy of love, of being seen, of being adored, and cherished.

Self-Loathing is a learned pattern of thinking and behavior created in your early environment from your parents' anger about themselves, whether acted out or not. It created a divided you and was done to protect yourself from future disappointment. It's based on the core belief you adopted as a child that there was something fundamentally wrong with you. You could also have encountered this from critical and shame-driven teachers or education systems that made you feel worthless or inferior if you didn't meet their standards of success. Indeed, any environment reinforcing the false idea that something was wrong with you contributed to this cavernous wound. In its extreme, you may feel disconnected from anything good, meaningful, and real, feeling hopeless, empty, and lost.

The good news is that you can overcome this feeling. You must become your own advocate. You are powerful and free to choose any point of view or any course of action that takes your side in your own life. You can learn to become more affirming, caring, and loving of yourself with your actions, behaviors, and thoughts. You give yourself more space to experience life from a compassionate and kind place of empowerment that lifts you out of the cavernous black hole you once lived into a brighter, lighter, self-affirming life that radiates your true wonderfulness.

I am a perfectly imperfect beloved child of this human family, and I love myself.

I love every part of what makes me who I am.

Deciding to love myself is a good decision, and I will reaffirm it each day.

"Self-loathing is the silent hemorrhaging of the soul. You don't feel or see the life force fleeing until it's no longer there, and then, of course, it's too late." –Sarah Ban Breathnach

"Certain people give off positive energy, others negative. It's the quality of someone's being, a measure of the love with which they've led their lives. It also reflects the inner work they've done, their efforts to heal anger, hatred, or self-loathing, which poison us like toxic fumes." –Judith Orloff

"Nothing is loathsomer than the self-loathing of a self one loathes." –John Barth

MEPSS Activities

Mental – At the root of Self-Loathing is the belief that something is intrinsically wrong, bad, or defective about you. If you can, recall some hurtful phrases from your childhood that became false beliefs about you. Write them down on thin paper strips, then create a simple ritual of tearing, burning, or shredding to release them.

Emotional – Creatively express your Self-Loathing. Get a big sheet of blank paper, some colored crayons, pens, or markers. Begin by drawing yourself in your full self-loathing persona. Really get into it. Be bold, angry, critical, and let it all out on the paper, the words, the phrases, the feelings, the colors, and the energy that has been stored at the bottom of that cavernous wound. Be careful not to do any harm to yourself or your environment. Focus on getting it out on the piece of paper. And if you need to do it more than once to get it all out, do it until you feel some release of energy and the beginnings of peace and calm. Then take another piece of paper and draw yourself as a genuinely loving, caring, and compassionate person would see you. Compare the 2 drawings. How do they make you feel? What memories, thoughts, or sensations arise? You may want to write them down on the back of each drawing. You may also want to journal about them. Or you may want to talk about them with a trusted friend, therapist*, or mentor.

Physical – Focus on the things you love*. Choose one or two things and make time for them. Really enjoy them and take in the pleasure, joy, excitement, and feeling of power and peace they offer you. Replace an addictive, harmful, Self-Destructive behavior with one of these instead.

Social – Social media tends to reinforce Self-Loathing through a phenomenon known as toxic comparison. We see a finely curated version of other people's lives and don't see what is under the surface, so our comparison is a picture-perfect, untrue, unrealistic version of other people's realities. So, take a break from social media for 24 hours and see if you feel happier, more relaxed, and more productive.

Spiritual – Practice forgiveness* for yourself. Give yourself the same compassion* you would give others who fall short of their goals. Stop beating yourself up for mistakes and failures. Understand that you are human, and as such, are fallible. Claim your humanness and your human-mess. Practice accepting and seeing yourself as perfectly, imperfect and loved as you are.

Self-Loathing

Self-Pity

Self-Pity is the useless, destructive Self-Wounding of playing the victim that denies the gift of empowering thoughts about yourself to become the hero of your own life.

Self-Pity is spending too much time in exaggerated unhappiness over your own troubles and reinforces the sense of being a victim. You learned Self-Pity when you were young. It stems from a circumstance or situation in which you felt life dealt you an unfair hand and you found it hard or even impossible to accept a circumstance or situation. You were unable to put your own suffering into proper perspective. It becomes an unconscious way of avoiding taking responsibility for personal actions or decisions you made in the past. Deep down you don't believe you are worthy of love, and you make yourself the victim, feel depressed and gloomy, and desire to seek out the condolences or sympathy of other people to make you feel better.

When Self-Pity becomes a habit, it becomes addictive with a craving for momentary care, emotional pampering, and the pleasure of being supported by others. It becomes your worst enemy as it impedes your progress and growth and creates Self-Destructive cycles of Self-Sabotage and cycles of Self-Destructive behavior.

When you are full of Self-Pity, you tend to engage in extreme, dramatic thinking with nothing in between. You find it hard to laugh at life or yourself and often feel defeated. You tend to keep yourself isolated and independent from friends and family and focus on the past.

Feeling sorry for yourself is normal, and in some instances, Self-Pity can serve as a self-soothing mechanism to help develop acceptance of the difficulties and perceived failures in your life. We all get tired of having to look after ourselves or being on our own side, and it's easy to succumb to this kind of Self-Wounding, using Self-Pity as a way out.

Instead of throwing yourself a 'pity party,' you must face your circumstances, feelings, and perceptions that make you sink lower and lower. Instead, turn it into the Self-Wonderful gift of responding with empowering thoughts and productive activities that allow you to become the hero in your life.

I turn this time of suffering into one of resilience and strength.

I choose to become the hero in my own life.

I accept this situation as a gift with grace.

"Self-pity is our worst enemy, and if we yield to it, we can never do anything wise in this world." –Helen Keller

"Self-pity in its early stages is as snug as a feather mattress. Only when it hardens does it become uncomfortable." –Maya Angelou

"If you repeat your negative memories in your mind and feel self-pity, then YOU are both the abuser and the victim – not those who wronged you in the past. Your present and future will be happier if you take control of your thoughts." –Maddy Malhotra

MEPSS Activities

Mental – How long is your average 'Self-Pity party'? Every minute you dwell on Self-Pity, you delay working on solutions to your problems. To build up your 'I refuse to' muscles and learn to regulate your thoughts, complete this phrase with 20 circumstances or situations; "I refuse to (your Self-Pity thought), and instead I will (your new improved empowered thought)."

Emotional – Give yourself permission to exaggerate and laugh! Tell a story using the form of melodrama about one of your 'pity-party' stories. You are the hero; who is your villain? Make it a whopper, exaggerating the circumstances, reactions, and responses, expressing all the feelings, gestures, moods, and movements, and even make sound effects, booing, cheering, and hissing, so that you have the crowd hanging on every word, right there with you. As you tell it, notice the energy you are creating as you go along and how you feel at the end of the melodrama. Cheer for yourself, the hero! Notice how you made those shifts and note how you can do it again in real time when another Self-Pity situation arises.

Physical – Use the following exercise to stop Self-Pitying behaviors by unscrambling your brain and allowing calm energy to flow through your body. You can do it with your eyes open or closed whenever you need to settle and return to yourself in the present moment. Put one hand on your forehead. Put the other hand on your chest. Breathe deeply a few times in this position until you feel calmer. Then move the hand from your forehead to your belly. Breathe deeply a few times in this position until you feel a shift. Then say to yourself,' I now move on with commitment and strength.'

Social – It's hard to feel Self-Pity when you are busy helping those who are less fortunate than you. What is a cause that tugs at your heartstrings? Spend at least half of a day volunteering. Notice your demeanor, emotions, feelings, and thoughts throughout your time. What are three takeaways from your time volunteering?

Spiritual – Watch the news and focus on a story of real suffering. Become one of the people in the story and feel Self-Pity. Then, be that same person but this time, feel the situation from compassion*. Now, be that same person, but feel the situation with optimism this time. Compare all three. What did each feel like? What did you do to make the shift to compassion? What did you do to make the shift to optimism? What shifts can you use in your own life?

SELF-PITY

Self-Pride

Self-Pride is the Self-Wounding that wears a crown of royalty to overcompensate for the gift of accepting yourself for the perfect greatness you are, nothing more, nothing less.

Self-Pride can be either nurturing or poisonous. When nurturing, it feels wonderful to feel proud when you accomplish something great and be recognized for something well done. It comes from a feeling that you respect yourself and feel good about your accomplishments. When it becomes poisonous, it shows up as a feeling that you are more important or better than others. This kind of Self-Pride makes life unpleasant, especially for those around you.

Other Self-Woundings often drive unhealthy Self-Pride, Self-Doubt, poor Self-Worth, and shame. When you feel bad about yourself, you want to do anything to make yourself feel better, so you look at others' flaws to conceal your own and criticize others as a defense against recognizing your own shortcomings.

Unhealthy Self-Pride has a drivenness, the pressure to succeed at all costs and repeatedly prove it to yourself and others. You overvalue and give yourself too much credit for your accomplishments when they are only modest ones. You don't give others credit for helping you accomplish a task; you praise only yourself for its completion. And because you want to try things beyond your capabilities, you frequently fail at overly ambitious endeavors.

Unhealthy Self-Pride prevents you from acknowledging and accepting yourself as a human being, complete with the flaws and vulnerabilities that make you interesting and unique. Instead, you feel shame for who you are and cover this up by intimidating others and ensuring you are right. Or you might engage in antagonistic, antisocial, or rule-breaking behaviors. You tend to manipulate, intimidate, or coerce others. Your relationships tend to be more aggressive and competitive, although you prefer not to compete at all, and this makes it difficult to sustain intimate relationships, for nobody likes a show-off and know-it-all. Self-Pride disconnects you from others.

The opposite of unhealthy Self-Pride, healthy Self-Pride, is authentic. It's an accurate, realistic estimate of your abilities and is the true measure of humility, which in its healthy form, is an honest, fair, and true estimate of yourself. When you come from this place, you can motivate and inspire others to take the lead and join with them without any threat, competition, or animosity, and accept yourself for the perfect greatness you are, nothing more, nothing less.

I am proud of the accomplishments in my life.

I pride myself on being a person of integrity and inclusion.

I accept myself for the perfect greatness I am.

"If you are filled with pride then you'll have no room for wisdom." –African Proverb

"Awareness' will not arise where there is deceit along with self-pride (maan). If there is deceit with self-pride, then one can never see the self-pride." –Dada Bhagwan

"I believe in pride of race and lineage and self: in pride of self so deep as to scorn injustice to other selves." –W.E.B. Du Bois

MEPSS Activities

Mental – Self-Pride often shows up when we feel we don't know enough about a particular topic. Choose a complicated topic that you can't master and spend time learning a little about it. Be curious about the topic and let go of your need to 'know it all.' Feel good that you made the effort. Be okay that you know enough without having to know everything.

Emotional – Notice when the flair of Self-Pride starts to show up and what you do with it. Then trace it backward and underneath it to find the early wound and the need* that wasn't met for you. Now fulfill that need for yourself in a simple, loving way.

Physical – Self-Pride is attached to an exaggerated image of yourself. Have fun drawing an exaggerated caricature of all those physical parts of you that you tend to take pride in. And if you find that fun, do one of your character qualities, skills, and abilities you boast about using symbols or images.

Social – An appreciation for life and people removes the need to compete and defeat them. It allows you to work with others as equals. Cultivate equanimity, emotional stability, and composure, especially under stress, which allows you to work together as equals. Choose a person or group you have felt 'above" and see how many things you can list that you have in common.

Spiritual – It's not surprising that pride is one of the 7 deadly sins in early Christianity (with precursors in Egyptian, Greek, and Roman cultures), and one of the 6 poisons in Buddhism that harm our perception and behavior and is addressed in many other world religions and literature. The antidote offered by Saint Benedict in his *Rule of Life* is to practice true humility*, which he defines as 'A true estimate of yourself as God knows you to be, knowing your place alongside the rest of the human race in the universe, your connectedness and dependence on God for the little greatness you have, nothing more, nothing less.' Write or create a true estimate of yourself in whatever way works best for you.

SELF-PRIDE

Self-Punishment

Self-Punishment is the Self-Wounding that locks you in jail to try to reduce feelings of guilt and the need to suffer while denying the key to open the gift of forgiving yourself.

Self-Punishment is surprisingly common! Self-Punishment is based on the belief that you must suffer. It is a coping mechanism learned in early life that keeps you trapped in a vicious cycle of pain and suffering. You use it to reduce your internal feelings of anger, failure, guilt, rage, rejection, and shame to free your conscience so that you can continue engaging with life, restore your reputation, and preserve your standing in your family, groups, or community.

Self-Punishment doesn't solve any problems. You believe wrongly that by fixing the pain you are sufficiently punishing its cause – you! You start to think that you are the cause of the problem, and feeling good is inconsistent with your unhealthy self-view. You use Self-Punishment as a form of suffering to make you a better person as it purges the so-called undesirable aspects of yourself. You use it as an irrational defense against all the pain you encounter in life and turn your anger, rage, rejection, and resentment against yourself. You become trapped in a vicious cycle of twisted codependence or even addiction. Pain does not solve the problem!

It's an unhealthy and harmful way you feel in control of your life. It continually leaves you beaten down, depressed, dejected, distracted, isolated, and weighed down by the continual Self-Punishment and other Self-Woundings you do to yourself.

Practicing Self-Punishment can become extreme and manifest as emotional suffering or mental or physical punishment. The physical side of Self-Punishment overlaps with the Self-Woundings of Self-Harm and Self-Injury. And in general, all Self-Punishment diminishes the Self-Wonderfuls of Self-Esteem, Self-Empowerment, Self-Respect, Self-Worth, and many more.

When you accept the key to open the gift of forgiving yourself, you can free yourself of your Self-Punishing tendencies from the past. You will benefit in many ways, including having clearer boundaries, greater Self-Respect, increased Self-Discipline, a quieter, non-punishing mind, better motivation to pursue your dreams and goals, and above all, pain relief!

I accept and love myself just as I am.

I am filled with love and affection.

I stop harmful and punishing behaviors and replace them with loving, caring ones.

"Release old concepts and energies that keep you in self-punishment patterns. Release old stories and create from a place of love and self-validation. You are worth it!" –Gautama Buddha

"Just do your best – in any circumstance in your life. It doesn't matter if you are sick or tired, if you always do your best there is no way you can judge yourself. And if you don't judge yourself there is no way you are going to suffer from guilt, blame, and self-punishment. By always doing your best, you will break a big spell that you have been under." –Don Miguel Ruiz

"The punishment imposed on us for claiming true self can never be worse than the punishment we impose on ourselves by failing to make that claim." –Parker J. Palmer

MEPSS Activities

Mental – Find a quiet place where you can relax. Ask yourself, "What would my life be like if I had a quiet, non-punishing mind?" What would it look like? What would it feel like? What would you let go of? What possibilities would open for you? What would you do? Who would you be? Choose one thing to integrate into your life right now. You can always add more. If you want, find a symbol or picture that reminds you of your quiet, non-punishing day.

Emotional – Find a picture of yourself as a 4-year-old if you can. Look into your eyes and see the beautiful, caring, innocent, loving, naïve, precious, and young human being you are. Now recall a time when your four-year-old self felt frustrated and upset trying to do something. Sense the emotions and see if you can identify which one or two are the strongest. Then find a way to gently release them by breathing gently out, doing the fingerholds* to shift the energy, or throwing a mini-tantrum in a private, safe space that releases all the pent-up energy. Spend time with that four-year-old child and share with them anything that might help them as they grow into the grown-up you and perhaps even beyond.

Physical – Explore the false mantra of 'no pain, no gain.' List 5 occasions when you have used this mantra. How did it help you achieve what you set out to do? If it did not help you achieve your goal, what happened instead? When has this discipline veered into Self-Punishment? How can you bring it back to being a discipline instead of Self-Punishment?

Social – When you are focused solely on your pain and Self-Punishment, it becomes magnified and separates you from feeling compassion* for other people's pain. What group of people suffering pain similar to the pain you feel can you direct your energy toward in order to feel compassion* and value their human needs. Find an organization that works to alleviate pain and suffering of this kind and do something to support it. When you support others, you will be supported as well.

Spiritual – What is one area or experience in your life that you would like to forgive* yourself for? What false beliefs or ideas are tied up with your refusal to forgive yourself? Counter each one with a new true idea or belief. Then go through each one and say, 'I forgive myself.' If you want to do more, give yourself a hug or even a kiss on some part of your body. If you need help, contact a spiritual center in your area that you feel comfortable with and ask for guidance and support.

Self
Punishment

Self-Righteous

Self-Righteous is the Self-Wounding that gives you the highest award trophy and excludes the gifts of openness and appreciation of other contributions and positions.

Self-Righteous is how you come across when you forcefully believe that your ideas and behavior are morally better than others. It's an antagonistic form of judging another that elevates you above another and makes you feel important while treating the other with disdain or disrespect.

When you are Self-Righteous, you go to great lengths to show others how good you are, but you come across as intolerant, manipulative, smug, with a 'holier than thou' attitude. You are no longer interested in hearing what anyone has to say if they present a different perspective or disagree with you, and you often express this in annoying, offensive, and overbearing ways. There is a forced quality that people push back against. There is no opening for authenticity, and psychological safety is broken. This leads to anxiety, depression, and guilt and causes many problems for individuals and societies.

Self-Righteous behavior is often a difficult trait to identify because it is not always expressed in a contrary or hurtful way. You may come across as Self-Assured and care about injustice, and you may not realize that you are Self-Righteous and off-putting to others with your rigid opinions and overbearing actions.

Self-Righteous indignation is evidenced by the rage caused by what is believed to be unjust treatment, such as aggression, hostility, intimidation, punishment, or violence done in the name of moral superiority. Another similar term — self-righteousness—is associated with a legalistic religious tradition. You trust in your righteousness and do not see yourself as a 'sinner' who has 'missed the mark,' but you easily point out the 'sins' of others.

Believing strongly in your beliefs, opinions, and values is important. However, there is a vast difference between the Self-Wounding of being Self-Righteous and speaking your truth with conviction. When you come from a place of conviction, you believe what you say to be true and are willing to debate, defend your position, engage in healthy dialogue, or speak up about it. You have the awareness, humility, and maturity to consider that you might be wrong and can look at yourself and self-reflect. This gives you the shared trophy that building strong and trusting relationships creates and offers you the gifts of openness and appreciation of other contributions and positions.

I accept myself and others as equally human, fallible, and loveable.

I open to and appreciate the gifts that others offer.

I am no better or no worse than anyone else.

"A self-righteous person is someone who always believes they are right and is more knowledgeable than everyone else."
–Marcus J Borg

'To love a person enough to help them, you have to forfeit the warm, self-righteous glow that comes from judging.' –Ron Hall

"Those who know their unworthiness seize grace as a hungry man seizes bread: the self-righteous resent grace."
–Randy Alcorn

MEPSS Activities

Mental – How is self-righteousness most often manifested in your life? Is it 'all or nothing' thinking? 'Black and white' thinking? Overgeneralizing? Jumping to conclusions? In any dichotomy there is a 'third way', the ability to look at things from a perspective that is creative and outside the confines of existing viewpoints. Brainstorm some 'third ways' for the pattern you chose above. What new space, ideas, or solutions were created? Choose one to use on your pattern. How will you apply it?

Emotional – Choose a particular person and describe the ways you feel superior to them. Write an apology to that person but don't send it. Instead, read it out loud to yourself and notice what sensations and feelings arise as you apologize. Then be gentle and compassionate with yourself, knowing that it is the abused, hurting, and insecure inner child that has used being Self-Righteous as a protective mechanism. Now, write an apology to yourself. Read it out loud and forgive yourself. End with a self-hug with both arms.

Physical – Where do you have the sensation of unworthiness in your body? Speak truth and love* to that part or area by saying, 'You are an integral part of my body and life. I accept you just as you are. I honor your function and appreciate what you do for me.'

Social – What are your favorite judgmental statements? What person or group of people do you direct them to? How does it make you feel? What does that feeling offer you? How can you get what it offers in a non-judgmental, loving, supportive way instead?

Spiritual – If you have a religious background focused on sin* rather than love* or are curious about new, more loving, and accepting ways of expressing religious or spiritual truths, check out a new spiritual center, church, temple, or mosque near you. You may look at their website, ask to talk with a leader or member, or read a book or other material that they recommend. What new insight motivates you to be more loving and less self-righteous?

Self-Righteous

Self-Sabotage

Self-Sabotage is the Self-Wounding of not voting for yourself that undermines the gift of your own winning success.

Self-Sabotage is engaging in thoughts or behaviors, often without realizing that they interfere with your longstanding goals and creates problems in your life. Self-Sabotage prevents you from living the life you hope, dream, and long for, leading to insecurity, resentment, and Self-Judgment.

Self-Sabotage is often driven by the critical, defeating, and unhealthy self-talk of the Saboteur* where you tell yourself things like, 'I'm terrible at this,' 'I will probably fail anyway,' 'I can't do anything right,' 'I'm not worthy' of something better or good, or 'no one cares.' These thoughts have no basis in reality, yet when you are prone to Self-Sabotage, they seem logical and accurate. These deep-seated thoughts and feelings fuel your fears and lead to other self-sabotaging behaviors. A succession of failures and disappointments creates further feelings of frustration and guilt, leading to shame, which continues your downward cycle.

Admitting to Self-Sabotage is the first step. This is painful, and you might avoid doing so for as long as possible or until you have no other choice. The key is to look at areas in your life where things seem to go wrong regularly. You can stop Self-Sabotage by monitoring your thoughts, beliefs, feelings, and behaviors and challenging them when they block your dreams, goals, wishes, or values. Shifting the Self-Wounding of Self-Sabotage by voting for yourself will lead you to the many Self-Wonderfuls you already have to create winning success and flourish in life.

Every day I feel more in harmony with myself.

My choices and actions are naturally aligned with my intentions and goals.

I can achieve anything I put my mind to.

"Self-sabotage is when we say something and then go about making sure it doesn't happen." Alyce Cornyn-Selby

"Our biggest enemy is our own self-doubt. We really can achieve extraordinary things in our lives. But we sabotage our greatness because of our fear." Robin Sharma

"Withholding love is a form of self-sabotage, as what we withhold from others, we are withholding from ourselves." Marianne Williamson

MEPSS Activities

Mental – Write down at least 5 things you do and can be proud of, even if they seem small or insignificant. Then compliment yourself for each one. Continue this practice daily for a week, a month, or even longer. Refer to your lists often until you can sincerely compliment yourself and receive compliments naturally from others.

Emotional – Think of a time when you let your anger get the best of you and didn't get what you wanted. Go back and revisit that situation. Notice the trigger that set off the anger, and this time, choose another, more healthy emotion to use instead. What new outcome can you feel good about and celebrate? Celebrate in a way that is fun and fulfilling for the new you.

Physical – What is something that you have avoided so as to not appear as a failure? Draw a big tic-tac-toe grid* in the center of a piece of paper. Place this incident in the middle of the grid. Look at it and practice getting comfortable with this failure. What did it take from you that needs to be restored to you in a healthier way? Add what you need to the squares around the center. Now re-frame each one into a possibility, a probability, or an opportunity to do instead next time. You might even take time to do one now!

Social – Look at your relationships. Is there one relationship in particular where you have a pattern of picking fights, leaving, or acting out? Replay it now in your mind and ask yourself – What makes me feel I must pick a fight, leave, or act out? Make a list of these triggers to have available for next time. The next time you face this pattern, slow down the interaction in your mind by taking a 30-second pause before responding. If you need even longer, then take the time you need. If you need to let the other person know what you are doing, tell them when you will return to continue the interaction. Then do what you need to do to take care of yourself in order to respond from a more loving* place. Each time you practice, you build a new pattern that will make responding easier from this new, more loving, intentional place.

Spiritual – This exercise starts with the end goal – What would your complete happiness look like? Dream away. Let the possibilities come, and don't let your Saboteur* voice try to talk back to you or talk you out of any of them to eliminate your future happiness. Keep them coming. Make a list of 50, 100, or more. Make them into a vision board or collage using words and pictures from print magazines or make a virtual collage using computer images and graphics. Keep it in a highly visible place in your home and pause for a minute or two each time you walk by to look at it. Remind yourself what you want in life and how you plan to get there. And if you feel really bold, share it with one or two supportive people who can help you stay accountable to your vision and goal of happiness in life.

SELF-
Sabotage

Self-Sufficiency

Self-Sufficiency can be a Self-Wounding when you refuse a helping hand; it is a Self-Wonderful when it's the gift of your own two hands providing for your own needs seemingly without help.

Self-Sufficiency exists on a continuum based on the natural desire and need to survive and reproduce as a human species. Self-Sufficiency is being satisfied and secure in who you are, your autonomy, potential, value, worth, and integrity. You naturally become more self-sufficient with age as you figure out who you are and what your purpose in life is.

When Self-Sufficiency is a Self-Wounding, it is unbalanced either to the extreme of not needing anyone or being so weak that you appear fragile, unstable, and unable to provide for your safety and survival. When Self-Sufficiency is balanced, it becomes a Self-Wonderful and shows a strong inner well-being and feeling complete in yourself.

American culture values independence and Self-Sufficiency, but practicing this extreme kind of Self-Sufficiency requires a lot of effort and energy. You may appear cold, detached, self-contained, and become so self-immersed that you behave selfishly without taking into account the needs of others. This kind of extreme Self-Sufficiency often results in depression, isolation, and feeling unsupported, not just by humans but by the unpredictability and instability of nature itself.

At the other end of the spectrum, too little Self-Sufficiency makes you dependent on others, fragile, ignorant, weak, and unstable, as though you are incapable of providing the basics of security and satisfaction with who you are and living a functional, interdependent life.

When you operate from a balanced sense of Self-Sufficiency, you enjoy being in charge of your life. You value authenticity, affection, friendship, and alliances that don't limit your freedom. You don't need to prove anything to anyone, and you respect yourself and others. You make your own decisions, are honest, and take responsibility for your failures and mistakes. You focus on your aspirations, desires, and goals, and what you can control and accept what you can't. You know how to face adversity, crises, disappointments, losses, and unexpected situations you can't foresee. You always try to survive any circumstance.

With the gifts of Self-Sufficiency, you operate from a healthy balance of confidence, emotions, independence, and optimism. You can rely on others, which all leads to feeling more empowered. The result is a feeling of fundamental wholeness and well-being that sustains you when you use the gift of your own two hands.

I am a Self-Sufficient person with the power to become who I want to be.

I can care for myself.

I support myself by asking for help.

"Sometimes God has to remind you that you're weak so that you can be set free from your 'self-sufficiency.'"
–Tullian Tchividjian

"The myth of self-sufficiency demands optimism without end, downplays life's challenges, and shames us when, inevitably, we fall short." –Ashton Applewhite

'Interdependence is and ought to be as much the ideal of humans as self-sufficiency. Humans are social beings.'
–Mahatma Gandhi

MEPSS Activities

Mental – There is something to be said about relying on yourself for your needs, especially during difficult times. Often this involves problem-solving in the moment. List 15 things you are prepared for in a natural disaster or emergency. List 5 things that you need more help with. Choose 3 of those things to get ready for when the time comes. What supplies do you need? Whom do you need to assist in any way? What do you need from yourself to increase your Self-Sufficiency?

Emotional – In what areas of your life are you doing too much by yourself? In what areas of your life are you relying on others to do things for you? When you feel like you have to be in control, what are your underlying motivations and needs*? When you allow others to help you, how does your Saboteur* voice make you feel? What is one thing you can do to balance your Self-Sufficiency?

Physical – What books have you read, movies have you watched, or stories have you heard from your family about bravery, perseverance, and Self-Sufficiency? What idealistic, unrealistic expectations might they mythologize? How have you bought into these myths in your own life?

Social – Go through your day and list 100 things you have because someone else did the work. You might be surprised at how little time this took! Now create a way to show gratitude for 10 of them. Be creative, and if the person who did the work is still alive, find a way to offer thanks directly. So often, people don't know how they have impacted others. Have fun!!

Spiritual – It has been said that the two most frequent prayers are 'help' and 'thank you.'

How have you been 'helped' by the Divine/God/Higher Power/Mystery/Spirit/Universe*? Who and what else was involved in answering each of those prayers? Write a personal note to one of them, sharing how much it meant to you. You can choose whether to send it or not. Show your thanks to the Divine/God/Higher Power/Mystery/Spirit/Universe in some meaningful way.

Self-
Sufficiency

Self-Torment

Self-Torment is the agonizing scream of a self-imposed Self-Wounding that denies the quiet gifts of comfort, delight, freedom, happiness, and other blessings of life.

Self-Torment is the way you torture yourself with mental pain or suffering, especially through your thoughts, by listening to the voice of your Saboteur or inner citric. These biting, cruel, harsh, punishing words with a sharp tone keep you in a state of doubt, criticism, guilt, judgment, and worry while reliving recent and past actions, memories, and other effects of toxic self-talk.

Self-Torment is often the result of old beliefs and habits you learned early in life. You were likely punished somehow when you were wrong, creating an automatic connection between a mistake and the penalty. You also may have believed that you had to endure some sort of punishment before you could be forgiven. And then, the pressure to be perfect magnifies your drive to get it right. Another way to motivate yourself to do something is by using harsh self-talk and verbal attacks. The impact of this illustrates how unlovingly and unkindly you were treated, leaving no doubt why you resort to Self-Torment.

Continuing actions and words of Self-Torment cause you to lose hope in the decency of life. You adjust and get used to it and continue to endure it without question. You lose compassion or empathy and go deeper into agony, despair, and dread. Self-Torment drives you to excess and makes you less human, like a dead person, not really living but detached and unresponsive to the goodness of life.

To shift Self-Torment to self-nurture, start making conscious choices to reconnect with compassion and nurture rather than torment yourself when you most need support. Pay attention to how you treat yourself, especially your self-talk. Just say 'NO' each time that Saboteur's voice starts the torment and torture. Permit yourself to be OK with forgetting things, making mistakes, messing up, and being unprepared for something unexpected. Begin to think of yourself as your own best friend, being compassionate, gentle, loving, patient, and supportive of yourself. Decide to direct love toward yourself and keep practicing this until it becomes your new default response and strategy.

Moving from the Self-Wounding of Self-Torment to the Self-Wonderfuls of Self-Confidence, Self-Esteem, Self-Love, Self-Worth, and so many others will silence the agonizing scream and offer the quiet gifts of comfort, delight, freedom, happiness, and many other blessings of life.

I listen to my inner loving voice.

I accept myself and create a peaceful, loving mindset.

I am free from my past guilt and shame.

"Who you are, in truth, who everyone is, is whole and perfect and beautiful.

And if that can be recognized, then it is possible that self-torture can stop!" –Gangaji

"Don't torment yourself with jealousy. It's a silly illusion that someone's life is better than yours, when the truth is that each one of us is on a different path." –Demi Lovato

"Everyone goes through hell, but not everyone stays there. Stop tormenting yourself by reliving the pain over and over. Good people go through terrible things, but wise people know when and how to let it go." –Bryant McGill

MEPSS Activities

Mental – Draw a cartoon of your biggest Saboteur*. Exaggerate this to a ridiculous extreme to express its drama and lies. Let it make you laugh! If you want, make cartoons of its circle of cronies and how they conspire against you. Have fun and let your laughter focus your creative energy away from Self-Torment and into something beautiful to use in the future. What did this experience show you about the drama and lies you have listened to? What was the beautiful message you found within it?

Emotional – Too often, you believe what others tell you so that you can feel love*. This form of Self-Torment offers temporary happiness but ends up wounding you as well. Imagine your favorite kind of pie. Now imagine eating a delicious piece of that pie. What are the initial tastes of love that you feel? Take another bite, this time tasting the lies you tell yourself so you can feel love. What are those lies, and how do they taste in your life?

Physical – Celebrate your awesomeness! Write down 50 great things you've done in your life. Now write 50 compliments about the things you've done. Keep these lists in your wallet or handbag to use whenever you need to feel good about yourself.

Social – How you treat yourself teaches others how you want to be treated. When you emanate a sense of fear, others can sense that energy of fear. What are you afraid of at the deepest level? List 10 ways you can counter this fear through the company of others. Choose one and do it!

Spiritual – Say 'Yes' as an affirmation of reality to yourself as a work in progress. Choose a past situation you still carry guilt from. On a piece of paper, make two columns. In the left one, write the rationally based feelings of guilt. In the right column, write the arbitrary feelings of guilt not grounded in fact. Use the list to write yourself a letter using your non-dominant hand* from Divine/God/Higher Power/Mystery /Spirit/ Universe*, who sees you as a perfectly imperfect beloved child, who understands that you did the best you could, and knows that you didn't know what you do now. Take as long as you need, savoring the love* that dissolves your guilt and Self-Torment.

SELF-TORMENT

Selfish

Selfish can be a Self-Wounding when you operate in a closed-loop system of Me, Me, Me, and the gift of Me when you openly care for yourself in thoughtful and loving ways.

Being Selfish isn't always a negative thing. It can be beneficial to be a little Selfish to take care of your mental, emotional, physical, social, and spiritual well-being to avoid burnout or overwhelm.

Being Selfish is a Self-Wounding when you are primarily concerned with your own personal pleasure or profit and disregard others. This is when being Selfish becomes a shrinking world. Soon, you are hardly aware of anyone else or anything else, just yourself. You often take more than your share without giving. You may be indifferent to the suffering of others and decline to help others if you don't feel like it. Most people dislike Selfish people.

Selfish behavior is usually a cover for a need that isn't getting met in a healthier way. Children are naturally Selfish, and part of bringing them up to live in society is helping them understand that other people have feelings and needs that must be respected. Some people are not taught this and therefore stay stuck here and act Selfishly. Sometimes elderly people can also seem Selfish when others in charge try to take care of them in a way they don't like.

Being Selfish is a gift when it arises from your concern for your own welfare and well-being. You take complete responsibility for your thoughts, feelings, wants, and needs. You strive to reach your full potential and focus your time and energy on advancing your own welfare. In fact, being Selfish may be one of the most effective ways to nurture yourself as you thoughtfully and lovingly take care of yourself. Coming from this place makes it possible for you to care for others in a Selfless way. Even Selfless caring and generosity are not really Selfless if it makes you feel good to do something for someone else! Instead of operating in the Selfish closed-loop system of Me, Me, Me, give yourself the gift of Me by openly caring for yourself in thoughtful and loving ways.

My journey to self-love isn't Selfish; it's about becoming the best version of myself.

I'm not Selfish if I focus on myself for a little bit. I must make sure I'm OK and healthy.

I am Selfish in the best sense of the word, thoughtfully caring for and loving myself.

"Selfishness is the art of losing friends and influence."
–Dale Carnegie

"All selfishness is based on the idea that I am separate from you." –Eckhart Tolle

"If we are not selfish enough to take care of our own health, how can we take care of anyone else?" –Dalai Lama

MEPSS Activities

Mental – Pick a day and make an intention to notice your thoughts. When you notice one that is Selfish, ask yourself if it is fully for your own profit or pleasure or if it is a thought that is speaking in a loving, caring, self-nurturing, Selfish way. Keep a tally of both kinds of Selfish – the wounding kind of Selfish and the gift of Selfish. Repeat often and try to tip the balance towards the gift of Selfish, and away from the wounding kind of Selfish.

Emotional – Underneath the wound of being Selfish is the desire to feel accepted, approved of, or valued. How have you tried to meet this need unsuccessfully through Selfish behaviors and actions? What are 2 ways you can better get this need met?

Physical – You must be Selfish enough to take care of your own health so you can take care of someone else. What are 10 ways you can take care of your own health as a gift to yourself in a gesture of love* and care?

Social – There is no question that you will encounter Selfish people! And you can choose to act in a Selfish manner in return or treat them in an understanding way. List 5 responses or actions you can use to help you not to take it personally and come from a place of understanding.

Spiritual – Your purpose on this earth is to help yourself work through the issues that further your personal growth and enlightenment. What arguments, barriers, conflicts, disappointments, trials, and upsets have shown up repeatedly? Choose one issue or pattern, go deeper, and ask yourself, 'What Selfish motives guided me?' Spend time discerning how to make amends, offer forgiveness* for yourself and others involved, and choose 2 things you can put in place to begin to act in a Selfless, more caring way.

SELfiSH

*Simply Self-Wonderful Resources

An asterisk * in the MEPSS Activities refers to more information and links here.

*Activities Referred to in the *Simply Self-Wonderful Inner Workout Book*

2-Second Rule – Receive, Pause, Respond - A small pause to take whenever you are about to indulge in 'bad' behavior or stray from the 'good.' This small break of 1-2 seconds can distract you from your current train of thought.

60-Second Technique – A 60-second countdown you start on your phone or watch whenever you feel the rush of emotion. Notice your body, your thoughts, and everything else about the experience. Do not attach any thoughts or stories; just watch them like 'passing clouds.' By the end of 60 seconds, the emotion and its hook over your behavior will have subsided and will be less central to your experience. By 90 seconds, the emotion will transmute into something else.

ACE Scores – Refers to the Adverse Childhood Experiences which occur before your 18th birthday. Your ACE score is derived from a short test meant for guidance and not judgment and shows how these experiences affect people and predict the amount of medical care that may be required as an adult due to them. ACEs include emotional, physical, and sexual abuse, emotional or physical neglect, having a caretaker, parent, or someone else in the home who is in jail, a substance abuser, or a victim of domestic violence, and the absence of a parent due to abandonment, death, or divorce. You can take control of your trauma*, build resilience, and live your best life by understanding your trauma and how to heal yourself and get the appropriate help from caring and knowledgeable sources. There are many quick and easy ACE quizzes online. One that is easy to read, take, and understand can be found at https://www.npr.org/sections/health-shots/2015/03/02/387007941/take-the-ace-quiz-and-learn-what-it-does-and-doesnt-mean

Acrostic – A type of writing in which the first letters of each line, word, or paragraph form a word or message. It is often used in poetry but can also be a memory device or word puzzle. They are entertaining and fun! Enjoy playing with them!

Archetype – Archetypes are archaic, universal patterns or images that derives from the collective unconscious and are the psychic counterpart of instinct. Archetypes influence 99% of human behavior. There are over 325 of them! See the full list at https://scottjeffrey.com/archetypes-list/

Autobiography in Five Short Chapters – A poem by Portia Nelson about how we progress and make changes to improve our lives and ourselves and how we gradually change attitudes and behaviors that are not working for us.

Body Language – Nonverbal communication based on posture, eye movement, facial expressions, gestures, mannerisms, touch, and the use of space. Watch Amy Cuddy's TED Talk, Your Body Language May Shape Who You Are https://www.ted.com/talks/amy_cuddy_your_body_language_may_shape_who_you_are/c

Boundaries – Invisible yet established property lines that separate your physical space, feelings, needs, and responsibilities from others. Your boundaries tell others how they can treat you, i.e., what is acceptable and what isn't. Without set boundaries, people may take advantage of you. You need to establish and proclaim your boundaries to set limits, express your needs, and create healthy, safe relationships.

Centering Prayer – A method popularized by Father Thomas Keating that opens you to God's gift of contemplative prayer. Best practiced in two short periods of prayer each day by doing the following: Start in a seated position. Set a time for your desired length of prayer. Choose a sacred word or phrase that reflects your intention. Begin your practice of silent listening and contemplation. Continue to return to God's presence when your mind wanders. End your time. For more, visit http://www.centeringprayer.com/

Chain Thought Bubble – The bubble used in cartoons to represent thinking, allowing words to be understood as a character's speech or thought.

Clifton Strengths Finder – Identifies your strength makeup as a leader. You can read more and take the hour-long assessment here. https://www.gallup.com/cliftonstrengths/en/home.aspx

Compassion – Caring about another person's happiness as if it is your own. It is not empathy, which involves responding to another person's emotions with similar emotions. It is not sympathy, which includes regret for another person's suffering. For more on Self-Compassion see **Kristin Neff**

Connecting with Your Divine Self – To connect with your Divine Self, set an intention to connect with it, be open to it, and receive its positive energy, love, inspiration, and all the awareness, gifts, and transformation it offers you. Let your thoughts go, and imagine that you are an infinite intelligence, unconditional love, and all-knowing wisdom looking out through your eyes. Bring your mind to a state of stillness and ask your Divine Self to make the connection. Release any thoughts, beliefs, or hesitancies that may hinder connecting. Then, if you want, ask for guidance, insight, or an answer as you enter into the silence. Be there as long as you wish as more love, power, wisdom, guidance, abundance, spiritual growth, and spiritual intelligence arise. After your time in silence, notice any new thoughts or messages that come to you. You may sense energy, peace, an inner knowing, an answer, or simply want to take a deep breath and release some old energy that no longer serves you. The insight, inspiration, or message will unfold at the perfect time. This does not have to be a long meditation and can often be done in 10-20 seconds as you pause briefly on a busy day to seek peace and ask for energy and guidance. Connect with your Divine Self often!

Delayed Gratification (see also **Marshmallow Test**) – The ability to put off desire or impulse for immediate reward. It promotes success in many areas of life and develops willpower, discipline, persistence, self-understanding, decision-making skills, and neural pathways. Trust plays a big role. Strategies include knowing your values, identifying your goals, eliminating distractions and temptations, creating a plan to break down challenges into smaller pieces, setting realistic deadlines, celebrating small wins by rewarding yourself, and practicing mindfulness to keep you focused and purpose-driven.

Deserve – Caroline Myss defines it as – "Do not use the word deserve. To decide who deserves what in the world positions you as judge and jury over others. When have you ever had all the facts? Never. That is a cosmic position only… Entitlement is a self-inflicted form of suffering." *Entering the Castle: An Inner Path to God and Your Soul, Free Press New York, 2007 p 343-4*

Divine Benevolent Source of Love – There are various names for God, the benevolent source of love and life, many of which enumerate the various attributes or qualities of a Supreme Being. You know this reality and can use whatever word works best for you Divine/God/Higher Power/Mystery/Source/Universe or something uniquely yours! In Judaism, the name is held in such reverence that it is not spoken. The Islamic tradition has 99 names for God. Explore the various faith traditions for more.

EFT – Emotional Freedom Technique (Tapping) – Developed by Gary Craig, it can help you let go of negative emotions, memories, and thoughts by stimulating (or tapping) specific pressure points on the body (similar to acupressure points in acupuncture), without having to talk about them. Very useful for unblocking emotions, fears, anxiety, emotional pain, anger, trauma*, traumatic memories, phobias, and addiction, as well as alleviating headaches and overall body pain. Bringing awareness to your unhealthy emotions helps release the emotional energy charge and promotes the healthy flow of energy in the body and mental and emotional fields. It can treat anxiety, panic, and any other stress-provoking emotion or thought. Adapted for simplicity and effectiveness from Gary Flint's protocol, here is the basic practice:

1. Think of an issue to work with and measure your anxiety level 0 (low) – 10 (high)
2. Tap the sequence 7-9 times at each point ending with saying, "In spite of the fact that I have this problem, I am OK; I accept myself."
3. Repeat the tapping sequence 2-3 times or until the anxiety level is 0-2.
4. Finish by rubbing the sore spot 3" below the collarbone and 3" on the left side of the sternum. For a demonstration by the founder of Capacitar International watch this video: https://www.youtube.com/watch?v=_92rfEmXKjA

Enneagram – Describes 9 patterns of how people interpret the world and relate to others. There are several schools of Enneagram thought, and the Enneagram Institute is a great place to start https://www.enneagraminstitute.com/. You can read through all 9 types and see which ones you resonate with then take the Riso-Hudson Enneagram Type Indicator to receive your probable type. You can also take other free ones, or buy a book with one in it, but this one is the most accurate. Recommended books are:

- *The Wisdom of the Enneagram: The Complete Guide to Psychological and Spiritual Growth for the Nine Personality Types*
  Don Richard Riso and Russ Hudson Bantam Books 1999
- *The Essential Enneagram: The Definitive Personality Test and Self-Discovery Guide*
  David Daniels and Virginia Price HarperOne New York 2009
- *The Enneagram Guide for Waking Up: Find Your Path, Face Your Shadow, Discover Your True Self*
  Beatrice Chestnut, Uranio Paes Hampton Roads, Charlotteville 2021.
  They also have a podcast series: https://podcasts.apple.com/gb/podcast/enneagram-2-0-with-beatrice-chestnut-and-uranio-paes/id1499745500

Faith – A word you hear thrown around all the time, faith is complex, misunderstood, and misused. Faith is a verb that works by love. You don't 'do' faith, 'be' faith, you 'have' faith. You have faith in something: yourself, others, God, the world, the universe, and even science, and others have faith in you. You will always have faith in something for, against, or a state in between. You have no other option. The very fact that you deny faith is proof of your belief in something. Faith offers a multitude of gifts, questions, and guidance.

Family Constellation Therapy – A therapeutic intervention developed by **Bert Hellinger** used to gain insight and information into a client's family history, dynamics, and possible dysfunctional patterns due to the broken love bond. It uses physical movement and positioning, often in a group setting to allow the interactions to arise.

Finger Holds for Emotions – A *Jin Shin Jitsu* self-help practice that is extremely simple yet profound. It involves holding each finger and thumb for 30 seconds to 2 minutes or until there is a shift in the pulsing sensation that balances and harmonizes energy in the whole body. The energy pathways running through the fingers are said to regulate over 14,000 functions within the body. Here's a video demonstration from Capacitar International's founder Pat Cane. https://www.youtube.com/watch?v=zC7PSJSoCwI

Finger Labyrinth – Like a full-sized labyrinth you walk through, this is much smaller and portable. You trace the path to the center using your finger. It helps calm your mind, body, and breathing and offers clarification or insight to a question or situation you bring as you trace it. To download a free labyrinth pattern (either the Classical or Chartres Drawing), visit: https://www.labyrinthsociety.org/download-a-labyrinth

Forgiveness – Forgiveness means different things to different people, but in general, it is an intentional decision to let go of resentment and anger. The act that harmed, hurt, or offended you might always be with you, but forgiveness helps free you from the offense, leading to improved health, healthier relationships, and peace of mind, and may even lead to feelings of empathy, compassion, and understanding for the one who harmed, hurt, or offended you. Along with the books listed above under People and Places: **Fred Luskin Ph.D., Colin Tipping, Desmond Tutu, and Mpho Tutu**, and the Tariq Khamisa Foundation offer peacemaking and restorative justice workshops and resources. Visit https://tkf.org/

Forgive Your Parents – You may want to forgive your parents for:
Raising you through their own unresolved trauma
Not being able to teach you certain skills, as nobody taught them
Not being able to understand you because they did not have the capacity
Raising you through their own fear, pain, struggles, and worries
Doing the best they could with what they knew and had
Following certain cultural norms that they were surrounded with
Being emotionally unavailable, as their parents were emotionally unavailable

Four Portraits – A Map of Conscious Thought – This may change how you look at the world forever! It can help you answer the following 4 Questions:
Who am I? – (First Person Realistic)
What do I want to become? – (First Person Ideal)
Who do others think I am? – (Third Person Realistic)
And What do others expect me to become? (Third Personal Ideal)
Here's the link to the article:
https://www.psychologytoday.com/us/blog/clear-organized-and-motivated/201507/4-self-portraits-make-us-self-conscious

Grace – simply put grace is Divine unmerited favor and kindness towards you. Alternately, the State of Grace is experiencing consciousness free from earthbound dualities as you live moment to moment. Frederick Buechner said it this way, "Grace is something you can never get but can only be given… There's nothing *you* have to do. There's nothing you *have* to do. There's nothing you have to *do*… There's only one catch. Like any other gift, the gift of grace can only be yours only if you reach out and take it. Maybe being able to reach out and take it is a gift too." For the full **Frederick Buechner** quote: https://www.frederickbuechner.com/quote-of-the-day/2016/9/9/grace

'Halo' Effect – A phenomenon in your mind when one thing casts a 'halo' on other things that leads you to believe that the latter has the qualities of the former. The 'halo' that our 'good' actions cast makes us completely delusional about the real impact of our choices and doesn't make any sense. This is how your mind works, and you often fall into this trap without even noticing it.

Humility – As defined by Joan Chittister: "True humility is a measure of self that is taken without exaggerated approval or exaggerated guilt. Humility is the ability to know ourselves as God knows us and to know that it is the little we are that is precisely our claim on God." *The Rule of Benedict: Insight for the Ages* Crossroads New York 1992 True Humility p 73

Imposter Syndrome – An internal experience of self-doubt, chronic feelings of fraudulence, inadequacy, and incompetence, believing you are not as competent as others perceive you to be despite your success in accomplishments, education, and experiences. This hinders you from achieving your full potential in your field of interest.

Inner Critic – see **Saboteur, Strategies for Responding to the Saboteur/Inner Critic**

Life Timeline – An easily visible way to get an overview of your life is to make a life timeline. It will take a while, so start with one category, then do it at your own pace until you feel it is complete (for the moment, anyway!). Here is an easy one to follow: https://www.createwritenow.com/journal-writing-blog/bid/94651/writing-therapy-exercise-make-a-life-timeline

Love – **As defined by Bell Hooks:** "Love is the will to extend one's self for the purpose of nurturing one's own or another's spiritual growth." Love is not an emotion. It is an act of the will that implies choice. And love can never coexist in a context where there is abuse. *All About Love: New Visions* William Morrow New York 2001, p. 4 via M. Scott Peck's book *The Road Less Traveled: A New Psychology of Love, Traditional Values and Spiritual Growth* Simon & Schuster New York 1978. See also **Gary Chapman** and **Barbara L. Frederickson**

Marshmallow Test (Stanford) - The power of delayed gratification* is best known by this experiment in the 1960s. It showed that delaying gratification is a choice of the individual, and delaying gratification improves your willpower and ultimately helps you reach your long-term goals faster.

Maslow's Hierarchy of Needs – Human needs* are met in a certain order beginning with physiological (survival) needs at the bottom of a triangle diagram and continuing up through safety, belonging (love), esteem (social), to the more creative and intellectually oriented 'Self-Actualization' needs at the top. Transcendence was later added at the top.

MBTI – **Myers Briggs Type Indicator** – Based on Carl Jung's theory of psychological types and developed by Isabel Myers Briggs, it measures psychological preferences in how people perceive the world and make decisions. There are 16 types resulting in a 4-letter code based on the dominant pair in each of 4 groupings: Extrovert/Introvert, Sensation/Intuition, Feeling/Thinking, Judging/Perceiving. To learn more and take the 'Instrument' (that's what they call the 'test'), visit https://www.myersbriggs.org/my-mbti-personality-type/mbti-basics/

Mental Health Professional and How to Find One – There are several types of mental health professionals and many kinds of therapy. Finding the right one for you is important. The right one is accessible, affordable, addresses your particular issue, and is someone you can be vulnerable with. It can be online or in person. It's not as easy as picking a name off a list, but often you can start there. You can consult your insurance directory to see which ones are covered by your medical plan, ask someone you trust to recommend one they trust, use a reliable online database and search by location, specialty, or other criteria, explore local resources such as community mental health centers and hospitals, which may offer affordable or sliding scale options, reach out to organizations that address your area of concern, such as anxiety, depression, food disorders, relationships, or trauma and ask for referrals or resources. If it is an emergency, call the new mental health hotline, 988, or the suicide prevention line, 1-800-273-TALK (8255), the Family Violence Prevention Center, 1-800-313-1310, or the SAMHSA (Substance Abuse and Mental Health Services Administration), 1-800-662-4357. Please don't wait; your beautiful and important life depends on it!

Mindfulness - Mindfulness is proven to offer significant benefits to your well-being. Mindfulness takes practice, and you can grow your practice by being fully present in the moment, aware of where you are and what you are doing, and not being overly reactive or overwhelmed by what is happening around you.

Mind Map – One of the best ways to brainstorm, capture your thoughts, memorize information, take notes, organize them, problem-solve, think creatively, and bring them to life visually, using paper, a whiteboard, a drawing app, or software. To create one, write the central topic in the center of a blank piece of paper and put a circle around it. Create your main branches with subtopics that are close to your central topic. Go deeper, look at each subtopic, and surround them with related facts, ideas, or images. Continue expanding each new subtopic until you fill an entire page or run out of words and images. Review your drawing and notice the denser areas and the sparser areas. You can find several videos detailing how to create mind maps online.

Needs – Underlying your actions, feelings, and thoughts are needs that must be fulfilled for you to be your healthy and truly unique self. You will experience anger, anxiety, conflict, frustration, and more when your needs are stepped on or unmet. See the **Nonviolent Communication** website for a list of human needs.

Neutral Separations - One of the easiest ways to discard **Other People's Energy** (OPE) is by practicing Neutral Separations, which distinguishes your Life Force Energy from OPE, empowers your personal energy and boundaries, as well as allowing greater objectivity and Self-Expression, thus creating a healthier, more harmonious relationship rather than unhealthy merging and draining of energy. It can also be used with people, organizations, and objects such as computers, etc., by following a Group Neutral Separations below.***

Neutral Separations for an Individual:

- Centered in your Meditation Sanctuary (the intersection of your ears and the top of your head) - intuit a person you choose to make energy separations from
- Greet the person spirit to spirit and hold an image, knowing, symbol, etc., representing the person outside of your aura (the energetic skin outside your body)
- Note 5 neutral, objective points of difference between you and that person
- Sense the uniqueness of each of you as individuals

****Neutral Separations for a group, organization, or objects such as computers:*

- Centered in your Meditation Sanctuary (the intersection of your ears and the top of your head) – intuit the group or object and simply place them outside your energy field on a bus, in a space capsule, whatever you imagine and create

Continue for both Individuals and Groups, Organizations, or Objects:
- Intentionally release their energy from your space and gift it back to them using the hand gesture of palms facing out, pushing toward them
- Intentionally call back your energy from them using the hand gesture of palms facing and moving towards you
- Receive your energy and draw it into your Life Force, receive it back into your body and ground into Present Time by using the hand gesture of palms facing the ground
- Acknowledge ending the communication by being silent for a few seconds
- Dissolve the image of the person/group/organization/object and release thoughts of that person/group/organization/object
- Reground in Present Time again, be in your Meditation Sanctuary and fill yourself up with your Life Force Energy ® Academy of Intuition Medicine, adapted by Judy E. Slater

Non-Dominant Handwriting and Conversation – Writing with your non-dominant hand accesses insights beyond linear and rational thought. You can use this technique for discovering subconscious and unconscious thoughts and feelings in conversations with the Divine*, uncovering creative ideas, intuition, journaling, problem-solving, and more.

Think about the topic you want to explore and write it down with your dominant hand.

With your non-dominant hand holding your pencil or pen, write down a response to your query. This will probably feel awkward and slow and is perfectly normal. As you continue, you will get better, and new ideas and thoughts will emerge to illuminate the topic. You can also try simultaneously writing with both your dominant and non-dominant hands to see all perspectives.

For a conversation with the Divine, use your dominant hand for your voice and your non-dominant hand for the Divine voice. Go back and forth until you have concluded your conversation.

Nonviolent Communication (NVC) – A process for supporting partnership and resolving conflict within people, relationships, and society developed by Marshall B Rosenberg, a psychologist, mediator, teacher, and author who wrote *Nonviolent Communication: A Language of Life* (PuddleDancer Press, Encinitas 2015). He founded The Center for Nonviolent Communication, https://www.cnvc.org/, and the San Francisco Bay Area Chapter, https://baynvc.org/. Both websites have a wealth of information, including the following free resources and more to download and use:

- *Feelings Inventory https://www.cnvc.org/sites/default/files/feelings_inventory_0.pdf*
- *Needs* Inventory https://www.cnvc.org/sites/default/files/needs_inventory_0.pdf*
- *How You Can Use the 4-part NVC Process* https://www.nonviolent-communication.com/pdf_files/4part_nvc_process.pdf

Other People's Energy - OPE – Every interaction is an exchange of energy. If not given back, it can lead to illness. You are meant to be 100% full of yourself (yes, pun intended; you can laugh). An effective way to get rid of OPE is by the practice of Neutral Separations*, creating a circle 8 with you in one circle and the other in the other circle then tracing the figure 8 until the energy is disconnected, creating an energy shield around your aura, create an energy drain with one arm extended towards the ground, or brushing the energy around you in downward motions and intending it go into the ground to be renewed and recycled.

Pleasure Principle – Coined by Freud, it is your most basic part of yourself instinctually seeks pleasure and avoidance of pain in order to satisfy biological and psychological needs. This driving principle makes it hard to delay gratification for the future yet unseen and even greater benefits.

Positive Distraction – A technique to shift your mind to something that holds your attention without causing stress and elicits positive feelings. They can come in many forms from art, digital interactives, games, imagery, music, puzzles, stories, toys, videos, and more.

Positive Replacement Behavior – Using a new helpful behavior to break and replace a previously harmful behavior pattern. It should be easy, rewarding, and satisfying and include **Structures** as a reminder. It may be incremental or all at once.

Saboteur/Inner Critic – Your Saboteurs are your inner critical voices shaped by painful childhood experiences and critical attitudes you were exposed to early in life that became engrained in you. At one time, they protected you against your power (which you were not allowed to express because you were a mere child), what you feared, namely rejection, abandonment from others, and, therefore, death (for when you were very young, you could not survive on your own.) Now grown up, the Saboteur tries to keep you small by reciting an old litany of judgments, limiting beliefs, and rules in the guise of protecting you from danger, loss of relationship or catastrophe. It uses 'shoulds,' 'oughts,' comparisons, the voices of significant people from your past, and societal norms and expectations. Your role is to identify these Saboteur voices that no longer serve you and act from the wise voice of your best and highest self to pursue your more fulfilling life.

Self-Forgiveness – An important component in healing your Self-Woundings and accepting all parts of yourself as Simply Self-Wonderful, to forgive yourself, you accept responsibility for what happened, treat yourself with compassion and kindness, understand your emotions and justifications for your actions, express remorse for your mistakes, apologize and make amends, look for ways to learn from the experience, and focus on making better choices in the future. Many of the **Forgiveness** books listed have a section on self-forgiveness.

Strategies for Responding to the Saboteur/Inner Critic – Never talk back to your Saboteur; if you do, this will engage you in a back-and-forth power struggle you will inevitably lose. Instead, acknowledge and name the Saboteur, using a lighthearted description of what it represents. By naming it, you tame it. Then address it and say, 'Thank you for protecting me in the past. I am in charge now.' Then you can ask it to leave and entertain itself somewhere else, like on a 'play date' until you are finished with something. You may never be able to keep the Saboteur's voice quiet and out of your life, but you will learn to recognize it for what it is, thus lessening its influence and increasing your power over it and your life. See also **Shirzad Chamine** and **Rick Carson**

Strengths Finder 2.0 – Gallup Press New York 2007
Now Clifton StrengthsFinder* website for online assessment is: https://www.gallup.com/cliftonstrengths/en/strengthsfinder.aspx

Sin – Defined here as forgetting your divine nobility in the lineage of love, the realm you were destined to from the very beginning. To be human is to be imperfect and perfectly loved. Beyond your 'sinfulness'; or missing the mark, you are a beloved child of the **Divine**. When you affirm the basic and inherent flaws of being human, you can accept a new way of freely living with your uncertainties, inadequacies, helplessness, lack of and failure of control, acknowledging that there is indeed something wrong with you, which is perfectly fine with the Divine. You were made that way on purpose; God is divine, and we are human with the divine spark that longs to belong to the Divine.

Structures – A structure is any device that reminds you to be in committed action and stay on track with your practice. They can be almost anything. The best ones are familiar, already part of your daily routine, appeal to the different senses, and are playful. Examples are setting an alarm, a picture or post-it note, a piece of music, a small token in your pocket, a particular piece of clothing or color, walking through a doorway, or getting in or out of your car. Your chosen structure will provide discipline and focus and create new habits in creative, fun ways.

Tic-Tac-Toe grid model – This is another form of the **Mind Map Model**, where you put an action you need to take, an incident, situation, or topic in the center square, then add what you need to do or look at in the surrounding squares. You can then make another grid for each of those depending on how much is needed, then work through each of the surrounding squares (and additional grids) until the center is resolved.

Trauma – Trauma has been used as a buzzword to replace everyday stress, and although all traumatic events are stressful, not all stressful events are traumatic. The experience of trauma is unique to each individual. You become traumatized when your ability to respond to a perceived threat is in some way overwhelming. It can impact you immediately or be hidden and not show up for years. Trauma is about a loss of connection to yourself, your body, your family, others, and the world around you. It can happen slowly, and adaptations take place, which are often sufficient until another trauma triggers it. Trauma is stored in the body, and body-based trauma-release techniques are the best way to deal with trauma. Being able to label it is helpful, although talking about it often makes it worse by re-stimulating the emotions and feelings that brought the original overwhelm in the first place. Understanding your **ACE Scores, Capacitar International, Emotional Freedom Technique, Bert Hellinger's Family Constellation Therapy, Peter A. Levine's Somatic Experiencing, and Mark Wolynn** are good places to start healing your trauma.

VIA (Values in Action) Character Survey – identifies your profile of 24 character strengths in 6 categories that make you feel authentic and engaged. Learn more and take the survey here: https://www.viacharacter.org/

Vital Practices – Expanding the typical spiritual disciplines to include other personal or communal activities you do daily or regularly that turn your awareness to the divine. They may look more secular than sacred, and they are absolutely necessary, important, essential for life, full of energy, and life-giving. When you aren't doing it, your spirit dies, and you feel dull, down, deadened. Vital practices change the heart. What makes your heart sing? What makes you feel fully alive?

Vulnerability – As defined by **Brene Brown:** "The definition of vulnerability is uncertainty, risk, and emotional exposure. But vulnerability is not weakness; it's our most accurate measure of courage. When the barrier is our belief about vulnerability, the question becomes: 'Are we willing to show up and be seen when we can't control the outcome?' When the barrier to vulnerability is about safety, the question becomes: 'Are we willing to create courageous spaces so we can be fully seen.'"
Braving the Wilderness: The Quest for True Belonging and the Courage to Stand Alone Random House New York 2017 p154

Western Medical Model vs. Eastern Medical Model – Both systems have different approaches, goals, and perceptions for treating disease and maintaining health. Western Medicine sees the body as a machine with standardized parts that are treated separately and can be replaced. It uses vital signs, general appearances, and laboratory testing for health examinations. It uses prescribed specific drugs to treat the symptoms. Eastern Medicine sees the body as a garden with interconnected elements and focuses on treating the whole person. It uses the elements of earth, fire, metal, water, and wood to interpret the relationship between the body and the natural environment. Many Eastern modalities measure the circulation of the vital force known as chi, or prana, by reading the pulse or muscle testing or stimulating acupressure or acupuncture points, and use this, combined with natural and herbal remedies, to treat the underlying cause. Naturopathic Medicine uses a system of diagnosis and therapeutics based on the patterns of chaos and organization in nature. It uses a variety of natural medicines and treatments to heal illness. In the past, these remained separate, but they are now being combined and referred to as Complementary Medicine or Functional Medicine.

Word Cloud/Word Cluster – A word cloud is an image composed of words in a particular subject or text, in which the size of each word indicates its frequency or importance. A word cluster is a group of words that share a common theme or global concept. There are many free word cloud generators you can use on the internet.

Zendoodle – The art of drawing designs using structured patterns concentrating on drawing small blocks of patterns at a time, going with the flow to create a work of art while deliberately creating a calming, Zen-like mood, focus, and state of mind. There are many websites featuring Zendoodles. You can watch a video of one being created, along with instructions here: https://feltmagnet.com/drawing/How-to-Create-a-Great-Zendoodle

*People and Places pivotal to my *Self-Wonderful* Understanding

Academy of Intuition Medicine® - official website https://intuition-medicine.org/
Francesca McCarthy, Founder and Director

Marcus J. Borg – His studies of the New Testament led him toward a deep belief in the spiritual life and in Jesus as a healer, prophet, and teacher. Pivotal books are: *Meeting Jesus Again for the First Time: The Historical Jesus and the Heart of Contemporary Faith*, HarperSanFrancisco 1994, and *The Heart of Christianity: Rediscovering a Life of Faith: How We Can Be Passionate Believers Today*, HarperSanFrancisco 2003

Cynthia Bourgeault – A masterful guide to Jesus's vision and traditional contemplative practices. *The Wisdom Jesus: Transforming Heart and Mind: A New Perspective on Christ and His Message*, Shambhala Boston 2008

Brene Brown, Ph.D. – for books, courses, podcasts, and more official website https://brenebrown.com/
The Gifts of Imperfection, Hazeldon, Center City, MN 2010
Cultivating 'Wholehearted Living' using 10 guideposts to help you let go of who you think you're supposed to be and embrace who you are.
Braving the Wilderness: The Quest for True Belonging and the Courage to Stand Alone, Random House New York 2017 definition of Vulnerability*
Daring Greatly: How the Courage to be Vulnerable Transforms the Way We Live, Love, Parent, and Lead, Gotham Books New York 2012

Frederick Buechner – Although he left this earthly plain in 2022, his voluminous work can be found at the official website for the Frederick Buchner Center https://www.frederickbuechner.com/
Wishful Thinking: A Theological ABC Harper & Row, New York 1973 p 33-34 Grace*

Rick Carson – For help with your Gremlins or Saboteurs*
Taming Your Gremlin: A Surprisingly Simple Method for Getting Out of Your Own Way, William Morrow New York 2003

Capacitar International – *Capacitar* teaches body-based healing practices that empower people to use their inner wisdom to heal and transform themselves to heal injustice and build peace in their families and communities. They work in over 45 countries and have a plethora of easy-to-follow materials and videos on their website, https://capacitar.org/

Gary Chapman - *The 5 Love Languages: How to Express Heartfelt Commitment to Your Mate*, Northfield Publishing Chicago 1992

Shirzad Chamine – For help with your Saboteurs* *Positive Intelligence: Why Only 20% of Teams and Individuals Achieve Their True Potential*, GreenLeaf Books Austin 2012
For information and programs, visit the official website, https://www.positiveintelligence.com/

Barbara L. Frederickson – *Love 2.0: Creating Happiness and Health in Moments of Connection*, Plume/Penguin New York 2013

Daniel Goleman - *Emotional Intelligence: Why it can Matter More than IQ*, Bantam New York 1994

Philip Gulley (first two with James Mulholland) – A Quaker minister and author, he writes of a loving God whose grace is unlimited and unconditional. His series *If Grace is True: Why God Will Save Every Person*, HarperOne New York 2003, *If God is Love: Rediscover Grace in an Ungracious World*, HarperSanFrancisco 2004, and *If the Church Were Christian: Rediscovering the Values of Jesus*, HarperOne New York.

Thich Nhat Hanh – A Vietnamese Buddhist monk, peace activist, poet, teacher, and author, he was a major influence on Western practices of Buddhism. Must-read books include *Peace is Every Step: The Path of Mindfulness in Everyday*, Life Bantam Books New York 1991, *The Heart of the Buddha's Teaching: Transforming Suffering into Peace, Joy, and Liberation*, Broadway Books, New York 1999, *Anger: Wisdom for Cooling the Flames*, Riverhead Books, New York 2001, *Living Buddha, Living Christ*, Riverhead Books, New York 1997 (with a 10th Anniversary Edition in 2007)

Rick Hanson – For books, courses, podcasts, and more, visit https://www.rickhanson.net/
Buddha's Brain: The Practical Neuroscience of Happiness, Love and Wisdom, New Harbinger Publications Oakland 2009
Resilient: How to Grow an Unshakable Core of Calm, Strength, and Happiness, Harmony Books New York 2018
Just One Thing: Developing a Buddha Brain One Simple Practice at a Time, New Harbinger Books Berkeley 2011

Louise L Hay – For affirmations, books, events, and wisdom from her life's work, visit https://www.louisehay.com/
Heal Your Body: The Mental Causes for Physical Illness and the Metaphysical Way to Overcome Them, Hay House Santa Monica 1982 – a classic to understand illness,
You Can Heal Your Life, Hay House Carlsbad 1984

Bert Hellinger – The original Family Constellation Therapy* located in Germany, https://www.hellinger.com/en/family-constellation/ use one of the several Mental Health Professionals* sites to find one trained in Family Constellation work

Camille Hamilton Adams Helminski – Student and teacher of the Quran and the Prophets *Ninety-Nine Names of the Beloved: Intimations of the Beauty and Power of the Divine*, Sweet Lady Press Louisville KY 2017

bell hooks – *All About Love: New Visions* William Morrow New York 2001 redefining love* as a verb that is sacred, redemptive, and healing.

Ernest Kurtz and Katherine Ketcham – *The Spirituality of Imperfection: Storytelling and the Journey to Wholeness*, Bantam Books New York 1992. This book revolutionized my thoughts on accepting myself as imperfect and perfect as a human being.

Amy Leavenworth – One of my energy healers who originally used the term 'Self-Wonderful' as a shorter way to name all the many selves we need and are already within us, instead of constantly naming them individually. With appreciation and creativity, I expanded this concept, and I offer it for your growth and healing.

Peter A Levine – *Waking the Tiger: Healing Trauma*, North Atlantic Books Berkeley 1997. Uses Somatic Experiencing to release trauma* from your body without talking about it. Website about Peter and his work, https://www.somaticexperiencing.com/home
Website to find Somatic Experiencing practitioners, https://traumahealing.org/

Fred Luskin, Ph.D. - *Forgive for Good: A Proven Prescription for Health and Happiness*, HarperOne New York 2002

Kelly McGonigal, Ph.D. – For books and more, visit the website https://kellymcgonigal.com/ *The Willpower Instinct: How Self-Control Works, Why It Matters, and What You Can Do to Get More of It* Avery/Penguin New York 2012

Kristen Neff, Ph.D. – Self-Compassion is defined by Kristin Neff as "a way of relating to ourselves with kindness, mindfulness, and common humanity when we experience pain or failure." For more about Self-Compassion and Mindfulness books, practices, resources, and workshops, go to her official website, https://self-compassion.org/ *Self-Compassion: Stop Beating Yourself Up and Leave Insecurity Behind*, William Morrow New York 2011

Carl Rogers - Unconditional Positive Regard is a technique used in non-directive client-centered therapy involving complete support and acceptance of a person no matter what that person says or does, permitting them to express their own experiences and feelings.

Rami Shapiro – A Jewish practitioner of perennial wisdom, the fourfold truth at the mystic heart of all religions, his books offer aliveness on the spiritual path. *Holy Rascals: Advice for Spiritual Revolutionaries*, Sounds True, Louisville CO 2017 and *The World Wisdom Bible: A New Testament of Global Spirituality*, Skylight Paths Nashville 2017 will take you to the heart of the world's religious traditions.

Colin Tipping - *Radical Forgiveness: A Revolutionary Five-Stage Process to Heal Relationships, Let Go of Anger & Blame, Find Peace in Any Situation*, Sounds True Boulder 2009 for courses, counselors, worksheets, and more at the official website,
https://radicalforgiveness.com

Desmond Tutu and Mpho Tutu - *The Book of Forgiving: The Fourfold Path for Healing Ourselves and Our World*, Harper One New York 2014

Francis Weller – *The Wild Edge of Sorrow: Rituals of Renewal and the Sacred Work of Grief*, North Atlantic Books Berkeley 2015, looks at the 5 kinds of grief using poetry and practices for deep healing. He offers workshops and more. To find out more, visit, https://www.francisweller.net/

Marianne Williamson – A spiritual leader who sees "Divine love is the core and essence of every human mind" and operates from that space. Perhaps her most famous quote is from her book *A Return to Love: Reflections on the Principles of "A Course in Miracles"*. You can find the complete quote here: https://www.goodreads.com/author/quotes/17297.Marianne_Williamson

Mark Wolynn – *It Didn't Start with You: How Inherited Family Trauma Shapes Who We Are and How to End the Cycle*, Viking New York 2016, for help with Family Constellation Therapy*

Enjoyed **The Simply Self-Wonderful Inner Workout Book**?

Buy the companion **The Simply Self-Wonderful Card Deck** using the QR code here.

Printed in the USA
CPSIA information can be obtained
at www.ICGtesting.com
JSHW051250241023
50732JS00007B/19

9 781961 757011